FROM CRIME TO CHRIST

COULD I HAVE SAVED ME?

FROM CRIME TO CHRIST

COULD I HAVE SAVED ME?

John "Little John" Paladino

*Foreword by Matthew Maher,
Speaker & Author of U MAY B THE ONLY BIBLE SOMEBODY READS*

Copyright

John Paladino, Jersey City, NJ

Copyright © John Paladino, 2022

All rights reserved. No part of this book may be reproduced in any form without permission in writing from the author. Reviewers may quote brief passages in reviews.

2022

DISCLAIMER

No part of this publication may be reproduced or transmitted in any form or by any means, mechanical or electronic, including photocopying or recording, or by any information storage and retrieval system, or transmitted by email without permission in writing from the author. Neither the author, editor or publisher assumes any responsibility for errors, omissions or contrary interpretations of the subject matter herein. Any perceived slight of any individual or organization is purely unintentional.

Cover Design, Editing, Formatting: Joanna Sanders, LLC www.colossians46.com

Scripture taken from the New King James Version®. Copyright © 1982 by Thomas Nelson, Inc. Used by permission. All rights reserved.

To Matt:

Words can hardly express the gratitude I feel in my heart for having met you. It is because of your outward expression of love for Jesus and your unwavering example to me, that I am now saved.

God's light through you, is what led me to Christ, even in the darkness. Thank you, my friend, for caring enough to show me this newfound faith that has saved my life.

I love you and cherish our friendship very much. My friendship and loyalty are yours for life.

Servus Servorum Dei

To Joanna, my editor:

Thank you for helping me take these stories from prison to paper.

~ John "Little John" Paladino

Contents

FOREWORD 1
INTRODUCTION 5
FIRST TIME STEALING 13
FIRST BREAKING AND ENTERING 23
FIRST STABBING 35
FIRST TIME IN PRISON: YARDVILLE 1983 41
CREDIT CARD AT MALL 59
SEASIDE HEIGHTS 73
GOGO BAR ASSAULT 83
SECOND TIME IN PRISON: SOUTHERN STATE 97
SMELL OF BLOOD 103
COLLECTING MY MONEY 113
MATTY 121
WHISKED AWAY 143
RELEASE FROM FEDERAL PRISON 153
FAMILY LIFE – TRYING TO DO GOOD 177
KITCHEN EQUIPMENT 181
I PULLED ME BACK IN 189
SECOND SWIPE 195

GET DOWN! GET DOWN!	201
QUESTIONING	209
COUNTY JAIL	213
CRAF TO MID STATE PRISON	217
SETTLED IN	223
I DIE!	229
LIFE AFTER DEATH	237
ABOUT THE AUTHOR: John Paladino	241

FOREWORD

"If you have any negative questions, comments, or concerns, please forward them to my Complaint Department. His name is Little John."

I often say that jokingly at my speaking engagements, and it certainly gets the audience laughing. At that point in my presentation, they are already familiar with Little John because I include prison drama stories that tell more than a few tense showdowns with gang members. Then, while in the middle of those stories, I suddenly pause and say, *"Oh yes, let me help you with the visualization process,"* at which point, I pop a prison picture of the two of us on the big screen. The audience reaction is always one of shock and awe, as they are transfixed by the sight of a fierce looking bald-headed, 330 lb. tatted up felon, and the image immediately drives the oxymoron home—that Little John's *not so little*— thus a better understanding of why I refer to him as my "complaint department."

What you need to know is that Little John was once a soldier for the Godfather, but as you will see by the conclusion of this book, he is now living as a soldier for God the Father. As I read through chapter by chapter, I was quickly reminded of how *only* Jesus can change the heart of man. Any man. Who has done *anything*! In addition, I was personally brought to remembrance of how God placed Little John into my life; first as a fellow inmate, then a loyal friend in a disloyal environment, and currently as a brother-in-Christ.

I will never forget how many times John reminded me of his calling for that season of life. He would tell me confidently, *"I firmly believe God has placed me here to safeguard you."* I don't believe either of us at that time fully understood the magnitude of that statement. But in hindsight, it is even more meaningful to see how God had His Sovereign hand on both our backs. Everyone in prison knew Little John was keeping a close eye on me and that kept so many shady characters from trying to turn their manipulative eye on me. John even wrote my mother a letter assuring her of my safety. He wrote, *"While I am in here with your son, you will never have to worry about a thing."* Can you imagine the solace that entered my mother's mind and heart after reading such words ... and then she saw his picture ... second thought, can you imagine the fear that entered my mom's heart? I'm joking obviously! But not really. One thing she knew for certain was that this inmate understood how to allay a mother's fear in the moment she needed it most.

At the conclusion of my school assemblies, where I tell my story of redemption, I designate the final fifteen minutes for a Q&A session. And without fail, the students are always most curious about Little John. I realize the obvious: it's because they are intrigued by his life of crime; and yet heard through my presentation of how he acted with such uncompromising integrity after his encounter with Christ. The students are blown away to conceive how this hard looking man can suddenly be guided by a humble heart. I guess integrity coming from someone who once lived a life immersed in criminal activity is intriguing. I guess transformation is what the heart of every soul craves. So many are fascinated at the radical change of someone who has clearly gone from crime to Christ.

In the pages of this book, you will get to follow John's harrowing experiences in the dark side of life. The sordid encounters

Foreword

John takes us through is not for the faint of heart. It is a glimpse into real-world depravity. You will read about a man who was hardened by the callousness of sin and whose actions took him in and out of prison and often without regrets. Yet within the script of each testimony, John creatively pauses and adds a hypothetical scenario of his salvaged-self who is making attempts to save his savage-self. It is fascinating to be privy to these encounters where *saved John* visits *lost John*. Obviously, his own attempts to save himself were futile (though make-believe) and God Himself would have to save John in the future.

This book chronicles the journey of a seasoned criminal's life, with all the resulting chaos and confusion, which supernaturally leads to the subsequent salvation of a lost soul. This book reinforces what believers in Christ already know and that is the truth that the Lord is always seeking to save the lost. It is a living testament of how God pursues us at our worst moments and in spite of our wretched past. John wants his readers to know that the Lord is in the business of saving those that the world labels as unredeemable. This book needs to be placed in the hands of anyone who thinks they are too far from God to be saved. It's a modern-day testament of how Christ can take a heart of stone and make that heart His home.

Imprisoned by peace,

Matthew Maher
Former Professional Soccer Player
Teaching Pastor, Coastal Christian Ocean City, NJ
Author of *U May B the Only Bible Somebody Reads*, *Imprisoned by Peace*, & *Unchained*.
www.TruthOverTrend.com

INTRODUCTION

I was born to a teenage couple, Elizabeth Bollinger and John M. Paladino, high school sweethearts from different towns. My father was a star football player and my mother was a Marilyn Monroe look alike. I suppose love was in the air back in 1964 because by September of '65 they found themselves in possession of an eight-and-a-half-pound baby boy, which they named John Anthony Paladino.

I vaguely remember my youngest years. I remember my parents and my newborn sister Christine, living with my mom's parents in a house in Hawthorne. My mom's folks were salt of the earth type of people. My grandfather, Clarence, "Sarge" Bollinger, was a veteran of World War II, the Pacific War. My grandmother, Francis Bollinger, formerly Higgins, was a newspaper woman. She worked at the paper in Paterson. My grandfather was from a German/Dutch Pennsylvania coal miner's family. My grandmother was of Irish heritage on her father's side and English on her mom's side. Her mom, my great grandmother Higgins, was my favorite woman next to her daughter, my grandmother.

Great grandma Higgins lived to be about 95. She was a very elegant old woman who dressed every day as if she was going out, kept a hankie in her sleeve, and sat in her throne of a rocking chair all day watching TV, sipping tea, and always wanting to read my tea leaves in the bottom of my cup. I used to sit and hold her hand and rub this mark which was something like a beauty mark on the back of her hand. By the time I was six or so we moved out of my grandparents' house and into an apartment complex in Jackson, New Jersey.

My grandfather's brother, "Uncle Buddy," owned all the garbage trucks in Jackson, as well as a cabana, which was a country club with pools, cabanas, and a golf course. He would have celebrities come and put on shows there. I remember seeing Tiny Tim sing "Tiptoes Through Tulips" while I was eating watermelon and jumping from pool to pool.

One day, myself and some other kids in the complex, being mischievous, pushed one of my uncle's dumpsters down an embankment. He came late that night yelling that "of all people, it had to have been my nephew." He made me climb down the embankment and then pick up all the trash that spilled out.

I had my first fight on the playground at those apartments. I remember playing on the slide, climbing up behind another kid who kicked back with his foot and kicked me in the face on purpose. My mother just happened to be looking out the window and yelled out to me to "kick his a**," which I promptly did. Later that night at dinner, the father of the kid came over and complained, and my father smacked me off the bench at the dinner table. He was a hit first, find facts second type of guy.

Although I had gotten in trouble several times prior to being sentenced to five years in a youth correctional facility (Yardville), I

Introduction

basically led a normal childhood in a household with both supporting parents, a sister and grandparents, who lived near me and my family.

I went to school, played with friends, rode my bike and motorcycle, did chores, watched TV, went to movies, roller skating, the park and celebrated holidays. My youth was spent happy and, for the most part, uneventful, aside from my personal adventures. I remember one time being so engrossed in the "Wolf Man" movie that my little two-year-old sister, along with our German Shepherd, Prince, left the apartment to wander around the apartment complex at night. It's hard to believe it was the 70's.

I was always getting into something. Once I tied a rope around a dead skunk's tail and dragged it home. (Definitely got yelled at for that.) Me and two Spanish girls had a little fort up on the hill behind the complex. My first near death experience was there, down by the embankment. There was an area that was much like a swamp. When I stepped into it, like quicksand, I sunk up to my neck before I got pulled out. I even lost my boot in it. I remember taking a bath and looking at all the mud in the tub.

As time went on, my parents bought a house in Lakewood and I went to school there. I had a crush on a couple girls, and I remember giving them quarters (25 cents) to get a kiss. I also loved my teacher, Ms. Brackston. My mom used to pick me up after school. My dad used to coach the Pop Warner football. I wasn't much of an athlete, and I had to play with the older kids because I was too big. I hated that. I tried playing the trumpet, that didn't work out either—the undecided mind of youth.

There were a lot of kids on the two blocks we lived on. We lived on north Oakland Street and a block over was Cherry Street. Both were dead ends. Eventually they built a bunch of houses, and a new little development about a block away. We would ride our bikes through there, run through the new construction houses, go to the field (football) for the high school at the end of my block, do all sorts of kid stuff. I remember a kid named Gary who lived across the street. Behind his house was all woods. He had a clubhouse and we hung out there a lot. These were the days before video games and computers. Our entertainment was playing outside all day long. Eventually people moved out, and new people moved in. Two sisters moved across the street into Gary's house, and I had a crush on them both. We used to flip baseball cards in front of their house.

While I don't remember much of it, most of my fifth-grade year was spent in the hospital for a sinus problem. During these younger years, my parents were fighting a lot and eventually split up. By the time I was a senior in high school, I had been moved around to six different high schools and moved back and forth between my mom's apartment, to my dad's girl's apartment, to a back room in my grandparent's house, and eventually back to my mom's apartment to finish up school in Asbury Park, New Jersey. I started to get into trouble; drinking, fighting, and smoking pot. In hindsight, maybe I was rebelling due to my parent's divorce. I can't say. During my last years of school in Asbury Park, I played football, and had about twenty scholarship offers before I was thrown out of high school for threatening the principal. I was a rebel without a cause.

I worked at the beach in the summer and also putting up fences for a guy named Steve Garrison before I was sent to a prison for the first time. After being released from prison, I went to live in Garfield, New Jersey, with my dad and my stepmom. My dad got me a job in the union as a carpenter, building high-rises in New York City. My first one was on 80th and Madison.

I worked, partied, sold coke and pot, and chased girls. I robbed, stole, fought, sold drugs, had sex and acted as criminally minded as I could. I eventually moved in with a stripper and continued on a path of destruction, until my grandparents got sick

Introduction

and needed help. I moved out of the apartment I had with the stripper and went to take care of my grandparents.

I lived in their basement, cooked for them, and took them shopping and at night, I worked in the city; taking the hour-and-a-half bus ride from Lakewood, New Jersey, to Manhattan every night. And in the wee hours of the morning, I'd take the bus back to my grandparent's house, make them breakfast, go to sleep for a few hours, and take them out if they needed to go to a doctor, the store, or a pharmacy. We'd have lunch and I'd chill and get ready for work again.

My grandmother was eventually diagnosed with cancer and put in the hospital. I'll never forget the call I listened in on, as my cousin called the house to tell my mom that my grandma wouldn't make it through the night. I hung up softly, so they wouldn't know I had listened, and just stood there listening to my mom's footsteps from above as she came to the basement door and called to me to tell me that my grandma might not make it through the night.

She asked if I wanted to go to the hospital. I went to get dressed and as I stood there looking into the mirror combing my hair, I turned and I knocked an old Bible off the dresser. The Bible fell opened up to Revelation. As I bent to pick it up, I read the first thing I saw and it was the vision of what Heaven looks like; how the streets are paved with gold and everything is jewel encrusted. I read in amazement knowing my grandma was going to this place.

I took that Bible with me that night. And although my grandma was in a coma when I got there, I sat there and read that Bible to her and told her where she was going. I know for a fact she heard me. She died that night and I was the last one to see her and it was the last time I picked up a Bible or wanted anything to do with God, for a long, long time.

My grandfather went to live with my mom in Florida, which left me all alone in their house. I continued to work in the city for a while, sold more drugs, robbed, and stole. I bounced at a few clubs and chased more girls.

Jail had taught me nothing other than how to commit more crimes. Entrenched with many layers of sin, my life was much like Dante's "Purgatory." I existed within a pattern of pushing boundaries, living on the edge, sometimes getting caught, and often going right back into the same pattern of behavior despite the consequences. I was in the same hell; just in different layers of it, depending on the season and the consequences at the time.

Many years later, asleep in a jail cell, I had an unforgettable dream; I wondered what it would be like if I could go back in time and talk to an earlier version of myself. I wondered what it would be like if I could talk directly to the kid who began pursuing trouble from such a young age. Knowing what I now know about the consequences that would follow my choices, I wondered if I could say what younger John would have needed to hear, at the time. Would any words, perhaps the words that I know now, have swayed me from these choices? Would I have had the arguments to dismantle my own rebellious way of life? I wondered if younger John could have been saved sooner?

The truth is, there is nothing that could have saved me except for God's grace. Had I experienced the consequences I deserved, you wouldn't be reading these words. By those consequences, my life was never meant to be lived. The breath I breathed was never meant to be inhaled. The blood that flows through my veins and into my heart was never meant to be pumped. My eyes weren't supposed to see, nor my hands feel. In essence, I was not meant to be. I was not living a life that was sustainable. Those four decades of life were to be extinguished, but for the grace of God.

Introduction

It is not my intent to dishonor anyone who has been involved in my story. Most names have been changed to preserve privacy. Some of the details are fictional; many are not. I've desired to give full glory to God by explaining just how low I went, and how unwarranted His grace was towards me. This is my story, but really, it's His. It's the story of the undeserved grace that took me from crime, to Christ.

FIRST TIME STEALING

I was running through the aisles of the ceramic supply store. The smell of baking ceramics was in the air, along with a thin cloud of ceramic dust. You could see the particles floating in the air, hanging in the rays of the sunlight that filtered through the windows. I slowed down near the back of the aisle. I was alone in a labyrinth; a maze of my fantasy world that I had now constructed for a personal adventure.

My mom was picking out supplies for her small studio in the basement of our house. She had run her own classes three or four times a week, teaching ladies how to paint gnomes, Hummel figurines and all sorts of holiday statues, plaques, and trinkets for a small price. While she was there for supplies, I was planning the takeover of this foreign planet, as the big bulging eyes of the rabbits, turkeys, Santas, elves, and Halloween pumpkins all stared at me. What was I to do? I decided I had to kill them for their belligerence toward me.

So, with a simple swipe of my super powered hand I broke them into pieces. Satisfied that my superhuman strength had accomplished its task I moved on to the next planet, (aisle), and continued my quest of total world domination, breaking things here and there. I moved stealthily through the maze of aisles until I came to a door; a doorway which opened to another world (an office). Even at the age of ten, my sense of right and wrong swept over me like a hot flash.

I knew I shouldn't cross over into this world, (into this office). I knew it was wrong. But like an explorer entering the tomb of a long-ago king or Pharaoh, I crept in, thinking at any moment poisonous arrows would come flying out of the walls to kill me. When that didn't happen, I assumed the floor was destined to collapse. Another step, no collapsing floor. Another step, closer and closer I came to the treasure chest (the desk). I stood before it as if I were looking at an actual chest of treasure. That feeling that had swept over me was stronger, but now it was coupled with elation, excitement, and adventure.

I reached out with my super-human arm that at the moment felt like it was a hundred pounds, my fingertips poised to grip the handle on the drawer, and I pulled lightly at the cold metal handle. The old desk, groaned as the drawer slid forward along the metal rails. A little more, I thought, and it would reveal its hidden treasure little by little. I pulled slightly harder each time until finally the drawer was opened. No hidden traps, no poisonous arrows, no trap doors in the floor to fall through. *I was safe.*

My eyes met the shining clasp of something. Paper clips, staples maybe. They glimmered from the fluorescent light above. Could it really be a treasure? I stepped toward it on shaking legs, thinking the worst. *I'll be caught by a tribe of cannibals who will roast my body and eat me for their dinner and later shrink my head down to the size of an orange.* But nothing.

I looked down into the drawer and it revealed its treasure; pens, pencils, tools for scraping the rough edges off the ceramics, paint brushes, paper clips, erasers, and some papers with writing and

First Time Stealing

numbers. *Could this be a treasure map telling me where the real riches lie? I don't know.* I reach to ruffle the papers when a voice behind me says "John." I jump and turn startled.

I started to say, "I'm not doing anything," but before I could, the man tells me, "Relax John. Don't be afraid. I just want to talk to you for a minute. Is that okay with you?" *I guess so.* I'm stunned, shocked, and embarrassed all at the same time, but oddly not afraid or scared of this man who seems familiar to me somehow. He sort of looks like my dad in the face and eyes, but this guy is much bigger, bald-headed, and has tattoos up and down his arms. I don't think I know him. *He doesn't look like a cannibal, so he probably isn't going to eat me or shrink my head, so I guess I'll listen.*

"John, you're not going to believe this, nor will you understand, so I'll keep it real simple and get right to the point. I am you at 41 years old. I've come back so I can give you a choice to make the right decisions about what you're about to do."

"What do you mean you're me? How do you know what I'm going to do? I told you already, I'm not doing anything."

"John, listen closely. You're about to open that middle drawer and find some envelopes and one has money in it. You're going to have to make a choice about whether you take it or not."

"Why don't you just tell me what I do, so I'll know what to do?"

"Can't do it, John, sorry. You have to act on your own free will. But what I want you to know, John, is this: You can do right because you know the difference between right and wrong, or you can do wrong and suffer the consequences. The choice is yours to make. But before I go, know this, John, God loves you and He would want you to make the right choice. I'll leave you with this to think about, a verse from Romans 2:18-21: "Know His will and approve the things that are excellent, being instructed out of the law and are confident that you yourself are a guide to the blind, a light to those who are in darkness, an instructor of the foolish, a teacher of babies, having the form of knowledge and truth in the law. You therefore, could teach another, do you not teach yourself? You who preach that a man should not steal, do you steal?" I know you don't get it all, John, but think about your choice and the difference between right and wrong."

"I don't know what you just said." I turn at a sound and turn right back. "Hey, where did you go? Mister, where are you?"

That was really weird. Didn't he say something about money? The top drawer slid shut easier than it opened. I better get out of here before the cannibals come. I think mom might be ready to go.

Every step towards the door felt like I was being pulled backwards by an imaginary rubber band. I looked both ways up and down the aisles of the labyrinth, no one in sight. *I can make my way out of here to the front and go home to ride my bike, enjoy my day, and play with my friends.*

My foot crossed over the threshold of the door opening back into the office and no sooner my curiosity turned me back around and in two steps I was back at the desk, with my hand on the cold steel handle sliding the drawer open and thinking of nothing but the treasure, and the riches that the weird man said would be there. This time, the drawer slid open without a sound and glided on its tracks with ease, although it felt slightly heavier.

It stopped with a clonk. I looked down to see a few envelopes sitting there lined up like little soldiers standing at attention. I reached for the furthest one. It was filled with paper slips with numbers on them. I put it back and grabbed the middle one. Same thing. Papers with little typed numbers. *The weird bald tattooed guy must have been lying to me.*

I put the second one back; I took the third envelope expecting the same result as the first two, with slips of paper with numbers. I opened it slowly like Charlie from Willy Wonka's Chocolate Factory opening up his Wonka Bar. I pulled back the flap and indeed, my golden ticket was there, only it was green. I pulled the bills out, folded them hurriedly and shoved them into my jeans pocket. I shut the drawer too hard in my excited haste and darted out of the office and back into the aisle of the maze. I practically ran to the front.

I stopped short right behind my mom who was at the counter paying for her supplies. She turned to me with a box in her hand and told me to grab the other box and follow her out. I picked up the box filled with small paint bottles, brushes, and sponges, and followed my mom to our huge suburban truck. She opened the side door, pushed her box onto the seat, and walked to the driver's side. As I slid my box on to the seat my senses were tingling. The sun was hot on my face, cars were zipping by, my senses were tingling.

My mom looked at me through her window as she opened the door. I felt as though she knew what I did. I felt like every time in every window of every car and business on that road knew I had just pulled off the biggest heist of the century. I was exuberant, excited and scared all at once. The whole ride home I stared out the side window trying not to confess to my caper. I could see my mom's reflection in the window. I turned to her.

"What?" she asked in response.

"I didn't say anything."

"Are you hungry? I'll make you a sandwich when we get home okay?"

"Okay."

I turned back to the window and the view of the houses and trees passing by at lightning speed. The whole ride home I could feel the money pressed against my leg. It felt like I had an actual brick in my pocket.

We pulled up to our house, got out, retrieved our boxes, and walked towards the back door which led to the basement. As I walked the sidewalk path to the back of our house, I was in front of my mom. My mind was racing. *Can she see my pocket bulging out? Am I walking differently, slightly to one side?* It felt like the longest thirty feet I ever had to walk. It felt as if the stupid money was pulling me down towards the ground.

I stepped aside while she opened the door. I went as fast as my feet could carry me down those fourteen steps, when I heard her voice, "John Anthony?"

"Yes?" in my head I'm yelling, *here it comes, she knows.*

"I'll be there in a minute to make you a snack."

"Okay!"

I run through the kitchen out into the living room, straight up the sixteen carpeted stairs to my room, slam the door shut, and pull the money out of my pocket. It falls all over the floor. I panic, scoop it up, and put it on my bed, and pull my blanket over it. I go to the door and I yell downstairs, "Did you call me?"

No answer. She must be in the basement still. I shut the door and pulled the blanket back to reveal my looted treasure. I sorted it out and counted it: 2 tens, 4 fives and 13 singles, $53. *I'm rich.* It's the most money I ever had in my life up to that point. It's 1977 and I'm rich. *But what can I spend it on? I don't have to buy food, can't drive a car, don't need clothes. I don't go anywhere except over to my friends and Friday we go skating. That's it. I'll buy soda and pizza at the skating rink and play pinball.* I take the money and hide it until the next day, which is Friday.

I woke up the next day, Friday morning, and pulled the money out of my hiding space at the bottom of my closet under my Monopoly game. *Okay, it's still there. No one took it or found my secret spot.*

I put it in my pocket, went downstairs, ate breakfast, said hi to my sister, and told my mom that I was going out to play as I ran out the back door. I grabbed my Apollo 5-speed bike and flew out to the driveway. I was almost to the street when my mom yelled out the window, "John!"

"What, Ma?"

"Be home by 4:30 for dinner when your dad gets home from work."

"Okay, Ma!" I took off, sped down the street, and totally forget about the money in my pocket. I spent the day playing, riding my bike, chasing girls, and jumping ramps. At 4:30 I was back home, eating dinner.

"Are you going skating tonight?" my dad asked over dinner.

"If I'm allowed, Dad. Can you take me?"

"Yes, I'll drop you off and get you at 9. Make sure you come right out, okay?"

"Yes, Dad."

My mom says, "Go take a shower and tell me what you want to wear so I can iron your shirt."

"Okay, Ma."

I went to the bathroom, stripped out of my clothes, and got in the shower. The water felt good. I could see the dirt coming off my body and swirling down the drain mixed with the soap. I heard the door open.

"I'm just grabbing your dirty clothes so I can throw a load in."

"Okay." I still wasn't thinking about the money. I dried off, got dressed, and went to my room to put my sneakers on, when my door opened and I looked up.

My mom was standing there with a weird look on her face. She looked angry and confused all at once. I looked down and see the money she's holding in her hand, my money.

She comes in and says, "Where did you get this?"

"I, I, I ..."

"Tell me the truth, John Anthony."

"I found it," I blurted out as though I was asking a question, as if I were asking her, will you believe this?

"I'm going to ask you once more, tell me the truth or I'm going to tell your father."

My first thought was to stick to my flimsy lie, but I thought better of that at the shear mention of my dad. "If I tell you the truth you won't tell Daddy?"

"I'll think about it. Now tell me where did you get this money?"

"I don't know what made me do it, but when we went to the supply place yesterday, I took it from there."

"I can't believe you did this! What were you thinking!"

"I wasn't thinking, I just did it. I'm sorry, I'll give it back. Please don't tell dad."

"John, I have to tell your dad you stole money. Stay in your room until we call you. I'm so disappointed in you."

My mom went and told my dad, who was very strict and very harsh with his punishments. He came upstairs and gave me a whooping with his belt and punished me for two weeks. No outside, no TV, no bike, no skating rink, no phone calls, nothing. I would just be able to come downstairs to eat and go back to my room. The next day my mom came and spoke to me to tell me how disappointed she was and how she was taking the money to the church to give to the poor box. I'll admit I cried because I felt terrible about what I did. I didn't want my mom or my dad mad at me.

Over those days of punishment, I kept thinking about that weird guy—trying to remember what he said, something about "he was me" and "do I steal or don't steal, make a good choice, God wants me to do good." *Oh, I can't remember! But that belt made me feel like I ain't stealing no more, that's for sure.*

FIRST BREAKING AND ENTERING

As a youth I got in stupid kid trouble like everyone else, but when I started to mess up in school, my parents decided to send me to a very strict Christian school. The principle was a man who literally could have passed as Hitler's twin, mustache and all.

The school was made up of about a hundred kids in total and it encompassed all grades. We had to sit at cubbyhole-style desks and do work from handbooks in all the basic subjects. I spent two to three years in that school and hated every minute of it. I felt restricted. I felt like I was being punished and I felt rebellious.

Needless to say, those feelings, combined with the hormones of a young teenage boy kept me from absorbing anything having to do with school, unless it had to do with girls.

Around this time, I experienced my first kiss and my first sexual experience. The moral challenges I faced at this age were confusing, complex, and compelling. I was young and foolish. Christianity wasn't taking hold of me. And although I went to Friday night youth Bible study and church on Sundays, my motives were always tied to girls and not God.

At this time, my parents owned a pizzeria called Big John's. We had a nice house, an in-ground pool, and my sister and I had basically whatever we wanted, except real supervision. My parents were always working, so we had lots of time home alone watching each other and fighting.

At some point around 1978 or 79 my parents separated and then finally got a divorce. This left our family broken and confused. I went back to public school and excelled at sports, including football and wrestling. I'd go skating every Friday night. I played sports and chased girls and occasionally got into fights. I was your typical confused and rebellious youth.

When my mom had to sell our house because she couldn't afford it anymore, my rebellion increased, and I got the bright idea to rob the next-door neighbor's house. They were nice people, foreigners from Europe somewhere. They had a huge German Shepherd that used to patrol their yard like it was a prison camp. He would run back and forth along the fence all day barking, growling, and snarling at anything that moved on our side of the fence. Over the years, that dog's four paws beat the ground down into a rut and over time that rut became a trail worn into the earth like a wrinkle on an old man's face.

As in my earlier years, I had no particular reason for this action. I had no wants, no needs. I didn't run with the bad kids. I had no catalyst for thinking about what I planned to do. I waited for my neighbor's car to pull out of her driveway. She left at a regular time every day like clockwork. Before leaving, she always left the dog outside to patrol the yard.

I went to the sliding glass door that overlooked our deck. I saw the dog running up and down his trail, watching, and looking for movement. I slid the door open on its track. It sounded like a huge grindstone crushing smaller stones into powder. I opened it enough

First Breaking and Entering

to slip out through the opening, stepped onto the deck, and down the five steps to the ground. I made my way to the fence at the side of our yard.

Leaves crushed under my feet as others fell from the trees in our yard. The ground was firm, the air fresh. I stepped nearer to the fence and the huge dog charged his side to show me that his territory would not be invaded without a fight. I raised my hands and yelled, "Get out of here, go!" and stomped my feet. The killer dog backed up. I yelled again, he scrambled back further. I hopped the fence and stood for a second to see if he would attack. He didn't and kept his distance.

I stepped towards the back door and slipped into the back foyer and closed the door behind me, so I couldn't be seen or attacked from behind. Inside, to my right was the door to the inner sanction. All I had to do was breech this door and I was in. But first, one more look to check and see if anyone saw me. I opened the street side door a crack and peered out of it with my face pressed against the edge of the door. No movement, no cops, nobody.

I shut the door only to be confronted by a big bald-headed man looking at me calmly and seriously. I was oddly calm myself, even though I realized I should have been scared, even terrified. But I wasn't. I stood in silence as He spoke.

"John, John, John," he said, shaking his head back and forth. I stand there stunned, mouth open, with no words coming out. I think I was in shock. *Where did this man come from? Was he in here already? He looks so familiar, like an old me. Am I dreaming?* Then his calm voice broke the silence like a hammer shattering a wine glass.

"John, I'm you. I've come here today to give you the chance to make the right decision. You know the difference between right and wrong. I know you can feel what's right in your gut."

I speak softly, almost in a whisper, "What do you mean you're me? Where did you come from? What do you want?" I want to run out the door, but I'm mesmerized by this man. I almost feel stuck in place, so I stay, and wait for his reply.

"I know you can't understand this, but I came to let you know that God loves you and has a plan for your life. God wants you to do good, John, and He wants you to make the right choices. In Deuteronomy 5:21 it says, "you shall not covet your neighbor's wife and you shall not desire your neighbor's house, his field, his male servant, his female servant, his objection, his donkeys or anything that is your neighbor's."

"I wasn't..."

I hear something outside and instinctively turn to peer out the door. Nothing, nobody is there. I turn with words on my lips, "...doing anything."

The man is gone. I think for a second that I have seen a ghost. I step towards the door I came in, through from the back yard, and I reach for the door handle. My hand clasps around the doorknob, and as I twist, I notice a small weed rake on the wall next to the door. Dried dirt is stuck to each of the three prongs of the rake. I let go of the doorknob and reach for the rake.

Its wooden handle has a piece of string dangling from it, which runs through a small hole at the end of the handle. I hold the garden tool with my right hand as I break off chunks of dirt with my left. The dried soil crumples to the floor in bits and pieces. A light cloud of dust floats down to the floor like it was blown off an old trunk in an attic.

First Breaking and Entering

I turned to the house door and slipped the prongs of the tool into the crack of the door right above the lock. The flat metal spaded tips fit in perfectly. I pry it back gently and hear the wood of the door make a slight splintering sound. I press harder and watch the door separate from the doorjamb. The door pops open, and I step inside, and look into the pristine living room. I notice the faint aroma of spices mixed with Pledge and the array of sun-cooked furniture. The giant plate glass window in the living room allows the sun to illuminate the room as if every light were on.

I pull the door closed behind me, but don't lock it. I am now standing in the living room of a house I have not been invited into. It is so familiar because it is the same layout as my house right next door. The only noise penetrating the silence of this house is the tick of the clock hanging on the wall. I don't know what I'm looking for, or even what I'll do when I find it. I walk from room to room noticing how those people have used their rooms, just as we did in our house, with a bedroom to the left, bathroom by the front door, kitchen off the living room, and the familiar stairs to the upstairs rooms.

I climb those stairs quickly and go into the room that would be my bedroom in the same layout. It's a room just like my own bedroom, only it's got different furniture, a desk, a chair, a sea trunk on the floor, and an armchair in the corner. I go to the desk, open the top drawer with pens, pencils, paper clips, all staring back at me. I shut it, go to the top of three drawers on the side. There is a coffee can which weighs a ton. I open the plastic lid, and find that it's filled with huge quarters. *Oh wait, I recognize these, they're half dollars or silver dollars.* I pick one out, it's a silver dollar. I take about ten of them and shove them into my pocket. I put the can back, check the other drawers, nothing good, some books filled with stamps and a lot of paperwork. I leave this room and go to the bedroom at the other end of the hall.

The bed is made, pillows perfectly placed. The room smells like my grandmother's perfume. I look in a few drawers, nothing but clothes. On top of the dresser is a jewelry box. As I open it, music starts to play. I instinctively slam it shut. I look up to see my face in the mirror. I look scared and out of place. I open the jewelry box again and I rummage through the rings, earrings, and chains, and pearls. I take two things that look real, a gold bracelet, and an earring with a diamond. I shut it and go back downstairs.

I check the bedroom off of the living room again. I take some knickknacks and leave. I close the door to the house behind me, check the back door to see where the dog is, and open it and step out. I jump the fence and I run into my house. No one's home; my mom is working, my sister is in school, and my dad has gone up north since the separation.

I went to my room to check out my stolen loot: Ten silver dollars, one bracelet, one diamond earring, and some knickknacks that looked expensive. I hid them all in my closet and waited for the fall out when, and if, they notice the missing items. It only took until the end of the workday before I was found out.

The woman came home, went into her house as usual, and within fifteen short minutes, a cop car was promptly in front of her house.

I watched the two officers walk up to the front door. I lost view of them from my bedroom window, which was situated smack dab in the middle of the house. I could only see about ten, fifteen feet past the corner of the house in either direction. My heart was racing. I was scared, but thought, *they could never know it was me, how could they?*

My mom was home by now cooking dinner and getting the house in order. My sister was in her room doing her homework. They were both oblivious to the thief in their midst; the one who had invaded someone's home, privacy, and respect. I stayed in my room, waiting it out.

Twenty minutes had gone by before the officers walked out. One went to the car, the other walked to the door at the end of the driveway, opened it, and stepped into the small area that I had occupied only a couple of hours prior. I watch him disappear into the door opening. I could see the bottom part of his body. I was transfixed on his black shoes. They were spotless and polished to a high sheen.

A light came on, but it wasn't the fire light of the tool shed. This light was dim and moved up, down, and side to side, like a flashlight. I sat and watched from my porch, waiting for the cop to step out and shine his light up at me in my crow's nest, but instead I saw the back door open, the door to the yard, the door I used to break the trust of our neighbor's bond.

The cop stepped out, looked around, over at our yard and house, then turned around and went back the way he came. The door shuts. A second later his shoes appear on the steps leading down to the driveway. He walks to the end of the driveway and stops. His partner meets him there and they talk for a minute. Then I notice the cop from the police car is the son of our neighbor across the street.

I watch their body language as they talk. They both turn toward our house. The officer from the tool shed slips the flashlight he's been carrying into a loop on his side, which is attached to his gun belt. It reminded me of a gun slinger holstering his gun, minus the twirling, spinning tricks.

Then they both take the first step toward my house. I couldn't actually hear their footsteps, but for some odd reason those four feet boomed like thunder as they lifted and hit the sidewalk. As they disappeared out of view the sound steadily continued in my head. I counted the cadence of their steps. I imagined they were at my gate within ten steps, and then six more to my front door. Just as the thought of them being at my front door came through my head, the ding-dong of our doorbell sounded through our house. Although it was a soft chime, to me it might as well have been as though Quasimodo was ringing the bells of Notre Dame, *bing bong*!

"Who is it?" my mom yelled through the house at the door.

And whoever stood on the other side yelled back, "It's the police, Mrs. Paladino."

I stood at the top of those eleven steps listening and hoping with everything I had that they were just going to ask if we saw anything, or if we were also robbed.

I heard the front door open and squeak at the halfway point, where it always squeaked. "Hey Paul, what's up? John's not home yet," my mom said, thinking they were stopping by to talk to my dad, who no longer lived with us.

"We stopped to talk with you, Betty Ann. Were you home all day? Did you see anything or anybody next door?"

"No, why, what's up?"

"The house next door was broken into."

"Oh my. Is Ms. Gorsky okay?"

"Yes, she came home to it. Can we talk to you outside for a minute?"

"Umm, okay." I hear the latch on the screen door click, then the squeal of the links and the screeching of the spring, then after it slaps shut, silence.

First Breaking and Entering

Fifteen minutes passed and I was nervous. Ironically, I wasn't nervous when I was in the neighbor's house uninvited, touching and taking things that weren't mine though. The silence was finally shattered with words I didn't want to hear. "John Anthony, get down here now."

I walked those steps like a death row inmate slowly, cautiously and unwilling to go to the door. My mom was standing right outside the screen as though the only thing separating her and I were a million puzzle pieces. "Yes, Ma?"

She steps in, followed by the cops. I walk to the living room. I can hear keys jingling. The screen door slaps shut and the crackle of the walkie talkies comes to life with random chatter I don't understand. "Car code 157 in progress, go to 372 Lincoln cop car 9." We all are standing in the living room. Suddenly, the room felt crowded.

My mom says, "John, do you know anything about what happened next door?"

"No, what happened," I say weirdly and nervously.

"Somebody broke in and took things from Ms. Gorsky's. You sure you don't know what happened?"

"No, I told you no."

I look at the two cops uneasily, then the one my dad knows steps forward and speaks to my mom first, then me.

"Betty Ann, do you mind?" She shakes her head no, he continues.

"John, listen to me. You know I'm friends with your dad, so I don't want to see you get in any trouble. We know you went into that house."

I look up in a shameful way, as he continues.

"We followed your footsteps from your neighbor's yard right to your deck. Where is the stuff, John? Go get it and maybe we can get Ms. Gorsky to not press charges." He says those words with a question mark hanging in the air. My mind is racing faster than I can keep track of my thoughts.

My mom breaks my thought as she grabs my arm, "What is wrong with you! Why would you do something like this? Where's the stuff? Go get it right now. I swear I'll call your father and he can deal with you!"

"All right, I'm sorry. I don't know why I did it." I half yell, half cry the words out, and run to my room. I get all the stolen loot together and bring it downstairs, the coins, the jewelry, the knickknacks, and hand it all to the cop my dad knows. He says something to me, but I just keep my head down. The only voice I hear is my mom's telling me go to my room and saying that she would deal with me later. Her voice is a mix of anger, blame, sorrow, and confusion.

I run up the stairs to my room two at a time, slam my door, and jump onto my bed and cry. I wasn't crying because I was afraid as much as I was ashamed for what I had done. I had no reason, no right, and no idea for why I did what I did. I felt sick to my stomach with regret.

Later that night my mom came to get me for dinner. She sat on my bed and talked to me at length about how I single handedly embarrassed her to everyone on the block. She talked in circles,

First Breaking and Entering

sometimes blaming herself and my dad for getting a divorce, and other times angry at me for doing such a stupid thing. She said she spoke to Ms. Gorsky, and that she didn't want to press charges. But my mom informed me that after dinner we were going over there so I could apologize to her for my blatant disrespect. And that's just what happened. I went and apologized after dinner.

Several months later, our house sold, and my mom, my sister, and myself all moved into an apartment on top of a music store in a small shore town.

FIRST STABBING

I heard my name being called from down on the street. "Little John. Yo, Little John, you up there? Yo, Little John."

I lowered the TV and went to the window. I looked out through the screen down to the street, to see my friend Kevin standing at the curb. He was standing in front of a '65 convertible Corvette. It was bright yellow with a white stripe down the side. He was smiling wildly.

I slid the screen up and leaned out the window, "Where did you steal that," I asked him sarcastically.

He replied, "It's my boy Joey's. He lent it to me for a few hours. Want to take a ride?"

"No, I'm good, I got to stick around, somebody's stopping by."

"What are you doing tonight, wanna hang?"

"Yeah, come back around 9:00 and I will be here waiting."

He said okay, jumped over the side of the car, and slid into the driver's seat. He revved up the car and burnt rubber onto Main Street, got to the corner, banked a hard left, and raced down the street on the other side of the baseball field that was across from my apartment. From my vantage point, I could see him speed down that street for almost two blocks. Kevin loved to go fast. He always had some kind of souped-up car and he loved to speed, speed some more, and drink cold cans of Budweiser.

I lived in the apartment with my mom and sister. We had moved to a shore town after my parents had gotten a divorce. I was only seventeen years old, and new to this town, but loving the atmosphere. I loved the beach and all the girls. My mom worked a lot, sometimes double shifts as a waitress and hostess at a restaurant a few towns away, which meant my sister and I were on our own a lot, especially on the weekends when the restaurant was busy. My mom worked two shifts to support us.

The one thing I loved most about living at the shore was the smell of the ocean air. Those sea breezes seemed to float through my windows all summer long, and cool things off, and make the air smell terrific. In the summer months, my days were spent at the beach swimming, chasing girls, and smoking pot. At night, I would head back to the apartment to shower, take a nap, and get ready to go out and hang at the arcade right across from the beach. A few friends and I would go to the corner liquor store before heading to the arcade. Since I looked the oldest, I'd go in and buy some beers for us or a bottle of Sambuca and we'd all go to this park called Green Acres and drink, then walk to the beach, and hang at the arcade.

We'd fight with rival kids from the arcade down the street or we'd pick fights with guys coming to and from the nightclubs that were at either end of the town, sometimes robbing them for money and jewelry. I sold pot and Mescaline. Sometimes we'd just steal what we wanted, food, beer, liquor. The cops were too busy watching all the nightclubs to worry about us, so we ran wild during the summer months. Winter was different.

Kevin came back that night with his sister and another girl he knew named Diana. He was interested in Diana and I liked his sister, Katie. I invited them into the apartment. We hung out, drank a little, and dropped a few tabs of Mescaline. After a while we decided to take a drive, so we got into Kevin's car, picked up more beer, and drove around town. I can remember sitting in the back seat with Katie looking out the window, seeing the light of the different arcades and businesses and watching all the people walking, talking, yelling, and laughing as they went about their business. I remember the world seemed to be going by in a blur.

I'd known Katie for a long time, and never tried to kiss her, but tonight in this back seat I decided to lean in and kiss her and she kissed back. Kevin found a spot and we parked. We sat in the car and drank some more beers, then we all decided to take a walk on the beach.

I took Katie's hand, Kevin took Diana's, and we all walked to the edge of the water. The waves were crashing on the shore. The air smelled like the ocean mixed with seaweed and a faint smell of fish. I could tell by the water line in the sand that it was low tide.

We got close enough to the water and were laughing and joking with the girls, threatening to throw them in. As all this was happening, I noticed a guy and a girl frolicking in the surf. They seemed to be having as much fun as we were. Katie and I walked up the beach a little, then back. We sat in the sand and talked. Kevin and Diana were doing the same a few yards away.

We watched as the guy and girl walked up from the water to a sheet they had set out. The guy started to accuse us of walking over his sheet and getting sand all over it. We all stood still as he walked towards us. He started to yell and scream. We argued back, saying we didn't know what he was talking about and just like that, he and I started fighting. Then Kevin joined in. I had the guy on the ground, punching him, and unbeknownst to me, Kevin stabbed the guy in the back.

Kevin jumped up and ran. Katie followed. Somehow, Diana and I just walked away. We didn't realize the guy was stabbed. He was yelling, his girlfriend was yelling, and she started following us. We got to the boardwalk, climbed the ramp, and just as we walked up to the boardwalk street level, a cop car cruised by.

While we walked across the street, I was telling Diana to remain calm and that if we got caught to just say we were just taking a romantic walk on the beach. As we made it to the opposite side of the street, I turned around to see the guy's girl following us and yelling, "Help! Help! He stabbed my boyfriend! Help, help!"

I turned to confront her. I was tempted to punch her, but I didn't. I know we should have just run, but we didn't, and now the cops were pulling up. The girl was still yelling that I had stabbed her boyfriend. I was saying that I didn't know what she was talking about. The cop called for backup and placed me in one car and Diana in another. The last thing I said to her was "Don't forget our story." I remember her looking like a deer in the headlights of an oncoming car scared, shocked, frightened and, like me, confused.

My confusion was lifted as the guy we fought approached the cops and he looked fine. But then he turned and lifted his shirt and there it was, a slash across the lower part of his back. His skin was opened like someone had unzipped him. It was about eighteen inches long and opened two to three inches wide. Surprisingly it wasn't really that bloody, it was just a gaping wound. As he pulled his shirt up the cop's reaction spoke volumes. He retracted from the sight of it and his expression was one of shock and disgust.

First Stabbing

I sat in the back of the cop car drunk, and high, and pissed off. The ambulance came, took the guy and his girl away with lights flashing and still I sat in the back of the cop car waiting. The cop got in and in silence he drove me to the police station with Diana and her cop chauffeur following close behind. We pulled into the police station; the cop cars parked side by side. I looked over and made eye contact with Diana. She was crying as she sat there looking scared. The officer exited her car and the two of them stood for a minute talking, then each of them came to the rear doors of the cop cars, opened them and told us both in unison get out and walk this way.

As I got out the cop placed his hand on my arm and walked me toward the door at the side of the police station. I noticed the other cop didn't put his hand on Diana's arm, just walked next to her as they went before us. As we walked into the station house, we were both told to sit in the few chairs that lined the wall. The lights seemed really bright and I squinted and adjusted my vision as I sat down. Diana seemed unphased by the lights as she too sat a seat over from me. The officer who walked me in pulled his cuffs from the black leather cuff holder on his belt. They made a click, click, clicking sound as he ran the cuff arm through the larger half circle the arm was attached to. "Give me your hand." I raised my arm as he placed the cuff onto my wrist. He closed it around my wrist, click, click, click, then placed the opposite cuff through a metal loop in the wall. I was now securely attached to the police station for safekeeping like a dog on a short chain in somebody's back yard. I wasn't going anywhere any time soon.

The police questioned me. And although I stuck to my story of being on a romantic walk on the beach, they didn't believe me and treated me as though I were Jack the Ripper. Diana was allowed to call her parents, who came and picked her up. And my bail was set at twenty thousand, with a 10% bond allowed. I called my mom, who came to get me the next day. My mom and my grandparents got a bondsman and bailed me out.

When I got home and told my mom what had happened, she was angry, but understood what happened. I placed several calls to Kevin, who finally called back. We spoke about our options and although he didn't want to tell the truth, he said he would take care of it and come forward.

A week went by and one night he called me and asked me if I wanted to go to Staten Island with him. He had just gotten a new motorcycle and wanted us to double up on it and take the ride. Between my concern at riding on the back of a motorcycle with him and being a little frustrated that he hadn't kept his word about coming forward to clear me in the stabbing, I refused his invitation.

Kevin spent the weekend on Staten Island drinking and getting high on dust. I forget now whether it was Friday, Saturday, or Sunday, but he and some friends got into it with some girls who left wherever they were and went and got a couple of guys who came back with baseball bats and machetes. Everybody ran and left Kevin, who by nature was a fighter, and probably knowing him, he tried to fight, instead of run. These guys beat Kevin to death with a baseball bat that day. Witnesses said they could hear the bat smashing his head in and hitting the concrete. He was murdered. At that time in my life, he was my best friend, and I still miss him to this day.

I got a lawyer and until this writing, never spoke of what really happened that night on the beach. What was I going to do, blame my murdered friend? I went to court and was sentenced to a five indeterminate. I did about a year and got out and afterwards went to live with my father in Garfield.

FIRST TIME IN PRISON: YARDVILLE 1983

I was in the Bronx the night before I was to be sentenced. I left work to meet up with a girl named Theresa to enjoy my last night before I knew I would be heading off to jail. I took the train to Pelham Bay and saw her waiting for me in her car with a huge smile on her face.

By the time I got the train from the Bronx to Manhattan to 42nd and 8th the next morning, to catch the bus home to Garfield, I knew I would be late for the sentencing, but I didn't care. I already knew I was going to prison. My lawyer had made a prearranged deal with the Prosecutor for the five-year sentence—five year indeterminate, which was anywhere from one day to five years. I would end up doing about fifteen months when all was said and done.

I got home, took a shower, got dressed, and my family and I hit the road. There wasn't much to talk about. We were silent for most of the trip. My lawyer briefed us when we arrived. By lunch time, we made it in front of the judge. As my name was called, I stood, and walked forward toward the small retainer wall that separated the audience from the judge, court clerks, sheriffs, and court stenographers. My lawyer already stood at the table reserved for the

Defendant and told me to sit down while he spoke with the Prosecutor. I turned in my seat to smile at my family.

They all looked worried for me, although we all knew the outcome in advance. I smiled and put on a strong face for them. The judge was announced and everyone stood as he entered. He came in, sat in his elevated throne looking down over the room, but more so, over the Defendant, me.

It didn't take long for him to get the proceedings underway. Before I knew it, he uttered the words, "I sentence you to five years in Yardville Youth Correctional Facility." The sheriff officer walked over and asked me to put my hands out so he could cuff me. I did as he asked while I looked at the faces of my parents and family. I asked if my dad could take my chain, and the Court Officer said yes. I bent my head forward and he took my gold chain and cross off my neck. My grandfather on my dad's side, who himself was no stranger to prison or the life of a criminal, winked at me and smiled. No encouraging words, no tears, no hugs, just a wink and a smile, which surprisingly gave me strength as the sheriff led me away through a door to the left of the Judge's elevated throne.

I was taken to a cell in a room behind the courtroom and put inside alongside several other guys who all stood there wearing orange jumpsuits. The cell doors slammed shut, metal crushing into metal. Cuffs were removed and I was left to fend for myself. I found a seat and sat down. I was now in the custody of the DOC, the Department of Corrections.

If you don't have patience before going to jail, you'll definitely have it once you get out. Jail is time spent waiting to wait some more. You wait to eat. You wait to sleep. You wait to go outside, wait to shower, wait for court, wait for visits, wait to use the phone, wait, wait, wait. A few hours later, the other guys and I were cuffed one by

First Time in Prison: Yardville 1983

one and led out to a van which was waiting at the sally port in the courthouse garage. We were loaded in and driven to the county jail.

As we pulled up to a fence, the officer driving blew the horn and the gates slowly rolled open. The driver pulled in and stopped at the next gate as the one that just allowed us in closed shut behind us. As one shut, the other opened. The driver pulled the van in and parked in front of a door. He and the officer got out, went up to the window in the wall and said something to whoever was on the other side. And just like that, a metal drawer slid out. It immediately reminded me of a bank drive through window. I looked to the right of the window next to the door and read a sign that stated, "no weapons beyond this point." They were checking in their guns.

The officers who seemed almost robotic in their movements and routines came back to the van, opened the side door and like sheep being led out of a pen, we all exited the van one at a time. I just followed suit and kept quiet. We stood in line in front of the door that buzzed and clicked. The officer who drove us, opened the door and said, "Come on, everybody, inside and don't talk."

We entered a whole new world. To me, the entrance should have had a sign over it like the one in Dante's Inferno, "all who enter abandon all hope." As soon as the door shut hard behind us, I felt different inside. No longer an 18-year-old kid with twenty scholarship offers to play football, no longer a son, a boyfriend. No longer anything but what I'd be known as from here on out, which was number 98463. My name would be secondary, but my nickname would become who and what I was, "Little John;" a lone wolf, a youngster ready and able to prove I could hold my own amongst the men who had made this their life.

The room we initially entered was "reception," minus the party. It was buzzing with activity. There was a large counter to my left, holding cells to my right, a shower curtain with who knew what behind it, and a room next to that with clothing bags hanging in it like at my dad's dry cleaners. Our names were called one by one. We were told to step up to the counter, where we were asked several questions, all done so mechanically you could tell it had been done thousands of times.

"Paladino, John?" I stepped forward.

"You Paladino?"

"Yes, Sir," I reply.

"You got any valuables on you, money, jewelry, watch, anything?"

I could smell his breath hitting me from across the counter, coffee mixed with cigar. He was an older man, way too overweight to do anything else except ask questions. "No."

"What is your date of birth?"

"9-15-65."

"Where do you live?"

I wanted to sarcastically say "here," but thought better of it not wanting to start off on the wrong foot.

"Garfield, New Jersey."

"What is your address?"

"47 Dawson Street."

"House or apartment?"

"House."

"You got a belt on?"

"Yes."

"Take it off, put it on the counter, then go sit in cell number one."

I undid my belt, which I learned is quite a task while wearing handcuffs. I slid it out of the loops and put it on the counter. I turned and walked to the cell numbered one, went in and sat down on the metal bench secured to the wall. As the officer processed all of us, that small cell filled quickly. The officers that brought us came to the cell and collected their cuffs and then another officer came and shut the cell door. Then we just sat and waited.

The guys in the cell started to become animated, talking amongst themselves and to other inmates who were mopping up outside the cell. Eventually one guy started to call to a cop out in the area where we had been processed, "Yo, Smitty, let us go back to the block, man. I gots things to do." Everybody in orange started to mock this guy and mimic him. "I gots things to do."

"Like what, go play cards?"

They all started laughing.

"Forget you, man. I'm hungry, I got me some store I wants to eat."

Another guy got up, went to the gate and started calling out to no one in particular, "Hey, let us get some bag lunches. They ain't feed us at the courthouse." The guards just sat there oblivious to the chatter and the requests. I just sat waiting to see what would happen

45

next. Finally, after what seemed like an eternity, (but was really only an hour and a half), a guard came over, opened the gate and told all the guys in orange to go back to their units. They happily scurried away talking nonsense.

"You. Come on out."

I got up and walked out. The guard started to direct me, first to the counter where I had left my belt, then to a small room where I was fingerprinted and photographed. After that, I found out that the curtain provided the changing room.

"Strip. Put your clothing in a black bag. Take the towel on the chair, and the soap, and get in the shower. Come out and put on the orange jumpsuit that will be waiting for you on the chair. What size are you? 3X at least."

He pulled the curtain shut and I did as I was told. I stripped, showered, and put on the orange jumpsuit as the guards milled around the counter area.

Once I was done, the guard came over, "Follow me." We went to a room down a hallway. "Grab a bed roll and a mattress." There, in a canvas laundry bin were blankets rolled up with sheets inside the roll. It reminded me of a huge swiss roll. I grabbed one and put it under my arm as I reached for the stack of battered two-inch-thick mattresses. I grabbed the top one, not realizing it was heavier than it looked.

"Come on, Paladino, you are going to B-1." I followed him down the hall through a door. We had to be buzzed through to go down another hall to a door with a guard standing outside of it. "Here's Paladino, bed B," He said to the guard at the door, then just walked away.

First Time in Prison: Yardville 1983

The guard opened the door with a huge key that reminded me of a skeleton key used for dungeons. The door opened and twenty different smells hit me at once. Bleach, body odor, steam from a shower, urine, feces, something cooking, paint, soap, and a few other smells I couldn't identify. The guard walked down a catwalk and I followed. On the left was a wall with barred windows, on the right were bars, and beyond the bars were metal tables, a blaring TV, and cells against the far wall. They were cut into the wall like little caves occupied by sea animals, only this was no zoo—at least not any traditional zoo. This was a zoo of a different sort. It housed men, most dangerous and deserving of a cage.

The guard walked down the dimly lit hallway and stopped about halfway, where there was another gate. He chose a different key from the loop. The huge keys were differentiated by colored tape at the base of the keys. The first was red. He opened the gate and told me I was in bed four. I stepped through the threshold, turned right and went through another gateway, only there wasn't a gate.

A few guys looked up from a stainless-steel table, where they were playing cards. I walked forward trying to look like I belonged. Aside from the TV, it was quiet. There were another two guys playing chess. I walked past cell one; it was dark but there was the form of a body lying on the bunk.

Cell two was the same, a dark outline of a body. In cell three I saw a red eye in the darkness staring out at me. There was smoke in the air from a cigarette. I got to the cell, where the number four was more like a U than a four. The bottom half of the number was peeled away. I stepped through the small opening sideways, carrying my bed roll and the mattress. It was too small for me, but I squeezed through and tried to find a light in the dark. A string dangled from above that I yanked lightly, and watched it dance and wiggle as the light blinked on.

My new home was an eight-by-four cell with a metal bunk bolted to the floor and a metal toilet on the back wall. Sticking out of the wall on top of the toilet was a small sink, sort of like the ones you find on a plane. There was nothing else. I threw my mattress on the bunk, threw my bed roll on top of the mattress on the bunk and sat on the edge of the bunk on my lumpy mattress alone.

At some point I laid down and dozed off. I woke up by somebody wrapping on my cell door frame, "Yo, my man, yo, my man, you eaten?"

"Yeah, what time is it?"

"It's dinner time, 4:30, my man. Come on."

He walked away. I got up, threw some water on my face and walked out into the dayroom I had entered through, which was now bustling with action. Where there were two guys earlier, there were now about twenty.

Guys were in line by the gate where there was a pushcart loaded with plastic trays. Each man stepped up and was handed a tray by an inmate on the other side. An officer stood a few feet away to the left. I got my tray and went back to my cell, and sat on my bunk. I opened it and was hit by a smell that was of no food I had ever smelled before. At first, I thought the stuff was bad, but I looked out to the tables and saw everybody eating it. Some guys were trading their meal for other portions of the meal, but for the most part, everybody was eating it. I picked up my spork and scooped up some of this brown-sauce-type-stuff along with some of the rice. To this day, I still can't tell you what it was or what half the stuff is that they feed you in jail, but on a scale from one to ten it was about a two. It suffices to stop the hunger pains.

First Time in Prison: Yardville 1983

My existence in the county was a learning experience. I learned how to jail. I learned the rules of jail and how to carry myself. I worked in the canteen packing bags with inmates' orders and basically waiting to be shipped out to prison. My wait didn't take too long, if you don't consider five weeks long.

One morning my name was called. "Paladino, pack it up. You're out of here on the Blue Bird." (Which meant pack my belongings and that I'd be leaving on the Blue Bird bus to prison.) We were strip-searched, redressed, handcuffed, shackled, and loaded onto a big blue bus.

The ride was uncomfortable, to say the least, but we made it to the prison in an hour and forty-nine minutes. The bus pulled up to a parking lot and stopped in front a building that looked more like a school than a prison. The only give-away was the fences with the barbed wire and the fifty-foot-tall watchtowers. Other than that, it resembled a school of some sorts on a farm-type landscape, with acres of grass, and trees set back on the perimeter of the grounds. There was a corn field across the street. It was actually picturesque.

The officers up front got off the bus, stretched, smoked and talked for a few minutes. A few others showed up from inside the building and then the officers who drove us, stepped back on board the bus and picked up a folder. "When you hear your name step up, spell it, and exit the bus. Line up on the yellow line outside on the sidewalk."

"Smith, Jeremy."

The guy in the third seat got up and waddled to the front. "Smith, Jeremy."

"Smith," he answered.

"Yes, Sir."

"Spell it and give me your date of birth."

"S-M-I-T-H, 7-22-68."

The officer ordered him off the bus. Out of the 32 inmates, I was the 17th to get off the bus after the same procedure. We all stood in line until everyone was off the Blue Bird. The officer at the front of the line yelled out, "Okay, listen up! Follow me into the building. Be quiet, do not talk, stay in line, do you understand?" We must have answered too timidly because he shouted again, "Do you understand!" In unison we all spoke out loudly, "Yes!"

We followed the guard into the building, and walked down the hallway to a rotunda, through a gate. After being buzzed in it seemed that this was the central hub of activity and the control center. Guards were in abundance, along with a lot of inmate activity.

We were told to stop and hug the wall. We lined the wall in single file, and once again, we were identified by name, date of birth and this time by our numbers, which were issued to us back in County. I was now recognized as inmate number 98463.

Guards started on opposite ends uncuffing us and taking our shackles off. You could tell by their speed and proficiency that they had done this thousands of times before. The chains from the shackles dragged across the floor. As the guards tossed them to the ground, our handcuffs were unlocked and dropped to the ground also. The sound of the stainless-steel cuffs and shackles being dropped and tossed aside reminded me of the scene in the movie, *The Christmas Carol* where the ghost comes to Ebenezer Scrooge at night and his chains rattled and made all kinds of noise.

First Time in Prison: Yardville 1983

Another guard picked up all the manacles and deposited them into a milk crate. We were directed five at a time to go to a door about ten feet from where we stood down the wall. "First five, go to the door where Officer Gonzalez is standing, get your issue and go to the back of the line. The order you were in will be the same when we're finished. Come on you five, let's go. One, two, three, four, and you, five."

This guard sounded like he was in the Army. He gave the orders as he walked up and down the line and pointed out the first five, as the rest of us just stood there waiting our turn to be the next five. By the fourth set of fives, I was the one going to get my issue, which from the looks of what the other guys had, was a laundry bag full of clothes, boots, sheets, a blanket, a towel, and a handbook.

I was the second in line but could see into the room where our issue came from. It looked like a mini sweatshop. There were shelves filled with brown uniforms and every other item including boots, blankets, sheets, handbooks, cups, boxes of plastic spoons, and forks. All these items lined the walls in the center of the room with what I thought were sewing machines. I soon learned they were stamping machines. Your name and number were stamped onto everything.

When I got to the door, an inmate asked me my name, number, and size. He picked up a laundry bag that was already half full of items, brought it to a table and yelled my sizes to another inmate, who took three pants, while yet another inmate grabbed three shirts, and yet another one selected my tee shirts and boxers. Within ten minutes, my bag was topped off and I was back in line to wait again until others were finished.

Once the process was complete, the Army guard yelled out, "Follow me! Stay in line and keep quiet!" We followed him around the other side of the control hub and down another hallway. Each of us now were in possession of a laundry bag filled with identical items, which varied only in size and the name and number that were stamped on them.

We made it to a gate. "Listen up! When I call your name, I'll tell you a cell to go to. Go to it and stay in it. Don't start wandering around or we'll find another cell for you that you're not going to like as much!" He called about six names and stated a number along with the words "top" or "bottom." At first, I didn't realize what that meant, but when my name was called, "Paladino, twelve top," I walked forward, went through a gate and walked down a short hallway, which had the cells on either side. I went to cell twelve and found out what "top" meant. The beds were bunk beds. I threw my laundry bag up onto the bunk and inspected the twelve by six cell: bunks, toilet, a small metal desk with a plastic chair, a window looking out onto a field, and a mirror attached to wall. That was it.

Now I got to wait to see who they were going to put in there with me. I peeked my head out the door and saw a little Spanish kid walking down the hall. He came to the door. I backed up out of the way, he stepped in. "What's up," he said.

"What's up," I replied. He put his bag on his bunk and then just laid down. I stood waiting for more orders, info, direction, but the only thing that happened was the Army guard came down the hall slamming cell doors shut.

Once he slammed mine, I was instantly hungry. "Damn, I'm starving," I said out loud, to no one.

"Yo, they gonna bring us food in soon, just chill."

Those words came from the shadows of that bottom bunk and that broke the ice enough for the introductions. "I'm Juan," he said.

First Time in Prison: Yardville 1983

"I'm Little John, Bro. What's up with this place?" I asked. And he explained to me that this was his second time here, and that this was a quarantine of sorts for him. We'd sit here for about three days, then they would filter us into population. Juan and I sat in that cell for three days. Three meals each day were brought to us, and we ate and slept those days away.

On the third day in the late afternoon a guard came by our cell. "Paladino, Ortiz, pack it up, you're going to general population." The guard went to a few other cells and did the same thing. I put all my belongings into my laundry bag and waited. About twenty minutes later, the guard came by, opened my cell, and said, "Go stand in the dayroom and wait for me to give you your housing assignment." Juan and I vacated the cell with pleasure. It's funny how happy you can be getting out of a cell after three days, but still be in prison.

The Officer sent out six other guys. The eight of us stood there while he went to his desk, picked up a sheet of paper and said, "Paladino, you're going to the north house. Ortiz, north house. Smith, south house. Baily, east house. Tucker, east house. Williams, west house. Johnson, west house, and Alvarez, you're in south house. Follow me, be quiet and stay on the right side of the hall at all times."

We walked down a long hall, made a left down another hall and came to a set of metal doors. The officer pushed us through them and we were outside just like that. I thought to myself, *Outside? Where am I, prison or not?* The metal doors opened up onto a huge courtyard. There were patches of grass in between the walkways that went left, right, and straight ahead. In the center of that courtyard was a handball court, a heavy bag, and a pull-up bar. Concrete benches were placed around the edges of the grass on the walkways.

At the moment the courtyard was empty, except for our group walking across it now listening to the guard give us direction. He looked down at his list, "Paladino, north house is over there. You and

Ortiz go to the north house and check in." As we walked away, I could hear him give similar instructions to Smith and Baily. Juan and I got to the entrance of a door marked in black paint as the North House.

Before I stepped through the entrance, I took a look around the courtyard and noticed the enclosing walls were actually the prison itself, with similar entrances spaced apart at different intervals; south house there, east house there, west house there. I also noticed slatted windows dotting the prison courtyard walls, which were the cells.

Juan and I went through the doorway where we found a desk. On either side of the desk were two dayrooms, with a few plastic chairs, an ironing board, and a TV. They were empty. I also noticed two sets of stairs on either side of the room we now stood in. They were marked "1 up" and "2 up," inferring that I now stood at ground level where "1 down" and "2 down" were situated.

"What is your name and number?" asked the guard who sat behind the desk.

"Paladino, 98463."

He looked at Ortiz, "And your name and number?"

"Ortiz 96274. I was here like two months ago."

The cop looked unimpressed. We stood there while the guard wrote a few things down, opened his desk drawer, took out a marker and wrote my name and number on an index card. He handed it to me saying, "Paladino you're in cell twelve, two down." He made another card, "Here, you're in cell eight-one up." He put his marker away, went to a board and pulled out a key, turned and handed it to me. "Don't lose your key or it's two dollars to replace it."

First Time in Prison: Yardville 1983

He walked to a gate set next to the dayroom, pulled out his huge skeleton key and opened the gate. I walked through and he shut the gate. I kept walking as I heard him say, "It's down on the right." I walked down that polished floor looking straight ahead, only glancing out of the corner of my eye at the doors I passed. The small window at the top of the door was empty in all except one.

A guy was standing in his cell looking out his twelve by twelve-inch window at me as I walked by. He nodded his head. I nodded my head back. At cell number twelve, I put my bag down. As I fitted the key into the lock it slid in with worn ease. I pulled it open, walked in and shut the door behind me, only vaguely remembering the cop saying something about shutting it because it was count time.

I now stood in a ten-foot by five-foot cell, toilet to the right, same mirror as the County, locker bolted to the wall, a single bunk on the left, and straight ahead was a slotted window looking out into the courtyard. I sat down at the small desk hanging from the wall and just let out a sigh, thinking to myself, *how did I get here?*

Once count was taken and then cleared, our doors were popped by the guard pressing a button by his desk. Everybody came out into the hallway, milled around and checked out the new guy, me. Some just walked by saying what's up, others stopped, introduced themselves and gave a brief itinerary of the day's events. Most had to go to work. I wondered what work here was like. I figured it couldn't be harder than building high-rises in NY.

I went to the gate and asked the guard if I could have cleaning supplies. He gave me a mop, broom, sponge, and some generic Pine Sol. I took it all to my cell and commenced to clean it from the ceiling to the floor, which took all morning. By lunch I found out we had to file out by housing units, walk across the courtyard, go in the building through the metal doors we came out of earlier and go into a huge mess hall capable of holding 300 men.

I followed the flow of people, learning on the fly as I went. I lined up like everybody else and waited patiently as the line inched forward to a slot in the wall. Each man stepped up to the window and each time a tray came out with food on it like a giant Pez dispenser. I got to the slot, received my tray, and found a seat.

The mess hall was alive with chatter, guys were all talking at once from table to table, some yelling, some talking quietly, and every level in between. It was a mad house. I ate and left. I went back through the metal doors I came in from and out into the courtyard, which was crowded with people.

I saw Juan, who filled me in on the inner workings of the prison. Apparently when it wasn't count or when you didn't have to be at work or school, you were free to stay outside in the courtyard and work out, play handball, or just enjoy the weather. At that moment, I chose to just walk around and try to get a feel for the place. Prison was a small world and I noticed that people were hanging around in their own social clicks. I met a few guys in the yard that I knew from the County, they in turn introduced me to their boys, and so on.

In a week, I was hearing my name being called out every five minutes as I walked around the prison. In a month, I was the man. Prison life wasn't so bad. It was like summer camp without girls. People still drank; in this case "hooch," which was homemade wine. They still smoked pot, took pills, and sniffed dope.

I chose to work out and learn a trade (masonry), so my days went by fast. I got visits on the weekends and just waited for my time to end. I was in and out in about eleven months. I had two fights, one in which I beat a guy with a shovel in masonry class for knocking over my project and the other on the unit, over some stupid argument I can't recall. Other than that, my time went well.

At one point I made it to the honor trailers outside the prison walls and worked on a detail raking leaves and doing grounds work at Trenton Psychiatric Hospital. I made it to a halfway house in Newark and worked at the airport buffing floors. Once I got released, I went to live with my dad and his new girlfriend and I went back to work in the city, where life went on.

CREDIT CARD AT MALL

The gym at the mall was very nice and my gold card allowed me total access any time I wanted to go. They had all the machines, free weights, and workout stations you could need. There was even an indoor track that circled the floor around the machines.

After spending months in the gym, going for three, four and sometimes five days a week, I started to notice some trends. Noticing things is what I do best. I notice when people make mistakes, when they forget to lock a lock, or when they forget to close a door, or take the keys out of the ignition. I notice all the things absent minded people forget to do.

I began to notice some men that would come into the gym, change into their workout clothes, put their street clothes and belongings into their locker, and go work out for an hour. So, I devised a plan to come to the gym around 4:30-5:00 p.m. right when most men would also be there. I'd sit in the locker room, acting as if I were leaving, while some unsuspecting man would come in, change and put his work clothes and belongings (beeper, wallet, keys etc.) into a random locker and never lock it.

As soon as they left the locker room to go and workout, I would open their locker, take a credit card or two, and their license. I'd go out into the mall and charge whatever I wanted. I would charge the items, run them to my car, come back to the gym, and replace the credit cards and license. I did this for several months—sometimes two, three cards a day.

All went well for several months, until one day as I sat there in that locker room a guy came in dressed in a nice suit. I thought to myself, *let's try Sak's today for a watch or necklace.* I smiled thinking of how easy this all was. The guy changed, put his stuff into his locker, and left the locker room. I looked around, my section of lockers was empty. I got up, went to the locker and grabbed the small latch that lifts up to open the locker. Just as I was lifting the latch, I heard, "John."

I turned with my rehearsed line on my lips, "Oh sorry, I thought I left my stuff," I cut my words short as I looked at an older me standing right in front of me. I was shocked, but somehow calm. It was almost as if I were sleeping or in a trance. Then the older me spoke again. "John, listen to me closely. I am you, I've come here to help you make a right decision. You know the difference between right and wrong and God wants you to do right. God loves you, John, and wants you to know He has a plan for you. All you have to do is choose to do right and accept His Son as your Savior. Listen to what He says in Ephesians 4:28: Let him who stole steal no longer, but rather let him labor, working with his hands what is good, that he may have something to give him who has need."

"What are you talking about? Who are you? Do I know you? God? I told you, I'm sorry, I thought this was my locker."

The older me speaks again. "John, you're not listening. I told you, I'm you, coming to tell you how to save yourself a lot of trouble and how to have a relationship with God. God just wants you to do good. He wants you to make the right choices so you can be close to Him and His Son."

"Excuse me, do you know if they give towels out in here?" A young guy had walked over and asked me this question.

I turned to answer, "I don't think so, sorry." He walked away and I turned back to the guy who looked like the older me, "Listen, I, ..." he was gone. I looked left, right, stuck my head around the lockers to the next aisle, nothing. Nobody was there.

I stepped out of the aisle of lockers and headed straight to the locker where the guy neglected to secure his belongings. I walked up to it, opened it as if it were mine, and reached for the pants hanging there on a hook by a single belt loop. I felt keys and change, in the front pocket, and a hard square in the back. I popped it out of the back pocket like a piece of toast coming up and out of a toaster.

I fanned through the cash and random bills in the billfold with my thumb; fives, ones, twenties, a couple of tens, and two hundreds, about $300 in all. I knew I could take it, but it would be noticed right away. What I wanted was a credit card or two and some ID, a license preferably. I shut the billfold and checked the small pockets on opposite side of the folds. Photos lined the other side in the small plastic lining. A couple of men and women standing on grass in a yard or park, hanging and looking happy, having fun, happy to be together. *Or are they looking at me and laughing knowing that I'll be caught because they have seen my face? Maybe I should take the photo and rip it up so they can't ID me. No, it's just a photo. Get what you came for, and let's go,* I say to myself.

I slide out an American Express card and pull out the license, memorizing my temporary name. I put the wallet back in the pants, the two cards in my pocket, replace the latch back to the up position, and close the locker. *Okay, remember 412, locker 412 second aisle to the right.*

My MO (modus operandi) was to go into the mall in which the gym was situated, charge several items, go to my car, drop off the items, come back into the mall, return to the gym, come back into the locker room and return the credit card and license all in a timely fashion, not to exceed the guy's workout, which I figured to be 45 minutes to an hour. Mission parameters set.

I went into the mall, which I knew intimately from scouting excursions and previous such adventures. I walked quickly to the Carousel (a clothing store), bought two leather jackets for around $500 each, then to Foot Locker and purchased four pairs of sneakers, two for me, and two to sell. I then go to Sak's and buy a Movado watch for a few hundred, all black, with a gold disk at 12:00.

From there, I quickly walked out to my car, and placed all the items in the trunk. I walked back into the mall, past a Radio Shack store and then I turned to go back, so I could grab a few things that I needed to do a bigger robbery: a police scanner, a set of walkie talkies, and a camcorder. I walked in quickly, found all the items I needed, and placed them on the counter. The whole time I was thinking to myself how close I was cutting the time, yet I proceeded not caring or heeding that inner voice.

Just as the guy was getting ready to ring the items up, a guy I know walks by and sees me in the store and yells out, "Little John!"

I look over, see him and quickly walk to him to avoid a scene. I say, "Hey man, I'm doing some dirt, don't call my name." He responds by telling me he just passed by some security guards who were on their way to the Radio Shack to arrest somebody.

I turned back into the store, went to the counter and I see the clerk looking at me suspiciously. "Um, there's a problem with your card, Sir."

I reply, "What's wrong?"

"It has been red flagged, and the credit card company is on the phone. They want to ask you your password." He says this as he holds up the phone in one hand and the credit card in the other hand.

I don't panic. I calmly reach for the phone with a "That's fine, thank you" on my lips. The clerk reaches forward a little more relaxed, looking like he was thinking that if I was willing to talk to the company, I must be the card holder. As he reached to hand me the phone, I snatched the credit card from his hand and swiftly walked out of the store.

"Hey, hey! Come back here! I called mall security..." he yells to my back. I'm already out the door and moving as fast as I can without running and drawing attention to myself. I speed walk out the door and turn right toward the exit door, which is at the end of the hallway. The exit door is like a small opening at the end of a huge tunnel. I take two steps and hear, "Excuse me, Sir, can we have a word with you?" I turn and I see four mall security guards. Without hesitation, I take off running down the well waxed, shining floor. My freedom is on the other side of that door, so I sprint like a bank hostage being freed from a bank robbery.

It seemed like the floor was moving beneath my feet as if I were running on a treadmill. The harder I ran, the further the door seemed to be from me. Finally, like a drowning man bursting to the surface after being underwater, I burst through the doors and out into the cool brisk air. My lungs burned with the overload of fresh night oxygen.

It was winter, dusk was falling fast. The streetlights with the parking markers on them were blinking to life. I ran as fast as I could out into the huge parking lot. I heard the mall doors slam open again as the security guards smashed through them like four linemen on a pro football team. I glanced back, they spread out like four horsemen trying to run down an escaped slave or prisoner. I thought of *Planet of the Apes* when the apes rode down Charlton Heston and threw nets onto him to capture him.

I made it into the secondary parking lot, and when I looked back, now I only saw two guards giving chase. I pressed on and made it to the outskirts parking lot, and onto the highway with no regard for my own safety. My safety relied on me getting away. The long leather trench coat I wore, flew behind me like Batman's cape. My dress shoes were slippery, not made for running, but I pressed on regardless. Cars started to blare their horns. I heard cars skidding, then a crash.

I jumped the highway divider and heard the one thing I did not want to hear, sirens. I looked back, no more guards. They fell away. They didn't have the incentive to press on that I did. I ran into the yard of a house on the opposite side of the highway from the mall's side. I ran to the backyard just as I saw the flashing lights approach.

The yard was half junkyard, half mulch pile. I stopped and surveilled the yard like a terminator with a digital display: junk car ten meters, garbage pile twelve meters, pile of leaves five meters, no life forms other than a squirrel that ran up a nearby tree.

If there's one thing I've learned over the years it's that cops look for motion. When they're driving their cruisers canvassing an area they hardly ever catch someone who hides, which is why, in that split second of time, I chose to bury myself under a pile of leaves and assorted trimming. I pulled my leather trench coat around myself and hit the ground quickly, entombing myself under the pile of wet leaves and brush.

The smell hit my nose and brought me back to my childhood when we used to jump into large piles of leaves in the fall. Everybody on my block would pile their leaves out in the street at curbside so the town could come and vacuum them up into one of their big trucks. As fast as that smell brought me childhood memories, the sound of walkie talkies brought me crashing back into reality, *I'm hiding from cops after being chased by four security guards from the mall for trying to steal more stuff.*

I knew I was just minutes away from being caught. I laid there trying to get my breathing under control. I heard keys jingling and a walkie talkie crackling. I heard leaves crunch under foot. I froze and held my breath and I exhaled with the greatest of care. My heart was racing, beating so fast as if it might break through my chest. I opened my eyes, but my vision was partially blocked by the leaves I'd covered myself with.

I saw movement about ten feet away, black boots. They looked like the boots of an Army soldier ready for inspection. They shined even in the shadows of dusk. "This is Smith, you see anything? Over."

"Nothing here, Smith. Stay put, he's here somewhere. Over."

"Roger that."

I knew my ability to outlast the cops had a lot to do with my freedom being at stake. I had observed that most cops just wanted to do their eight hours and go home. So, I laid there and waited. I heard a vehicle pull up not five feet from me. I couldn't see it but I knew it was a cop car; I could hear its muffled radio chatter. I laid there under the pile of leaves waiting for the cops, which were close enough to touch, to get tired, frustrated, or cold enough, to leave.

Every time I'd ever been in a situation like this, I would think of a soldier blending into his surroundings, either evading the enemy or waiting to strike. These same hiding and blending tactics had helped me before. My mind drifted to memories of past adventures where I had to blend into the brush or wait in the shadows. I know all too well how to be still.

According to my internal clock, about twenty minutes had passed when I heard leaves crunch and a voice over a walkie talkie again, "Smith, we're going to canvass the neighborhood. Come on back to the car, we're out front, over."

"On my way, over," I hear him say with a mixture of relief and frustration. He wants to catch the criminal, but he's tired of standing out here in the cold. I hear him walk away.

The footsteps get fainter as he puts distance between my hiding place and the corner of the house that he disappears around. I think I'm able to shift my body, so I slowly turn my head and rotate my torso in the opposite direction. Then I notice the tire.

The police van is still there, parked within feet of me. As I look up, I can see an officer sitting inside with his window cracked at the top, so the smoke from his cigarette can escape through the crack. I watch as that smoke wafts up from his mouth, moves like a snake, and climbs up and out the window.

He lifts a paper coffee cup with his other hand and sips it through the hole in the lid. Something moves behind him in the van. My eyes carefully follow the movement and I find a pair of brown eyes looking right at me, a black nose pressed against the window. It's a huge German Shepherd and he sees me.

Credit Card at the Mall

I'm as still as I can be, but he sees me, and I see him. It's like a Mexican standoff. We're officially in a staring contest—man versus beast. Who will blink first? Who will turn away first?

This police dog, who is probably a sergeant, has never seen a pile of leaves with eyes. As long as he doesn't bark and start to go crazy, I'm safe. Finally, after several excruciating minutes, I win the staring contest. Sergeant Dog blinks and turns his head. Must be a cat or squirrel that caught his attention. I don't know, but I'm thankful, because I was ten seconds away from blinking.

As I lay there my nose is filled with a mixture of smells, exhaust, cigarettes, dead wet leaves, and brush. I notice a red glow from the back of the van, then just like that it brightens. I know the driver must step on the breaks before he can put the van into drive. The van pulls slowly forward and the sergeant dog, who has reestablished eye contact, starts to drift forward with the van.

For a minute it's like watching relatives leave at Thanksgiving. I almost think sergeant dog is going to wave. We only break eye contact when the driver pulls far enough away to maintain sight. All I see is the taillights. Then nothing.

I laid there for what seemed like an hour. I could see the street beyond the back yard. It was lined with houses packed in close together. Small front yards with houses that were too big to be on them. Front porch lights were on and aside from a few cars passing by the street was deserted, except for the lone police car that kept circling the block like a great white shark.

I laid there and watched the patrolling cruiser come down the block and turn right. The taillights stared back at me like demon eyes in the dark. I started to count as I watched the pattern of his driving. *1,001, 1,002, 1,014, 1,015, 1,020.* I do this two times. The third time as soon as the demon eyes were looking back, I jumped up, start

67

counting and jumped the fence. I was in an open, vacant lot with overgrown grass, weeds, small saplings, and garbage strewn everywhere.

1,020. I hit the dirt knowing I had to take cover for a few seconds until the shark turned the corner. As I laid there, I looked up to get my bearings. I see a small square building. At first, I can't make out what it is, but then it hits me as the smell of steak, penne vodka sauce, and garlic float to my nose and let me know just how hungry I am.

I am determined to get inside, use the phone, get picked up, and make my escape, and maybe eat. The restaurant might as well be an oasis. I jump up, start to count, run forward. I make it three quarters of the way and hit the dirt again. I wait the few seconds again for the cruiser to turn and then I'm up and on my way once more. I hit the pavement running. Just passing the first parked car in the restaurant's lot, I'm almost to the door. I straighten myself out and walk in as if I'm a patron.

I walk past the coat check room in the small foyer and proceed to the huge dining room filled with tables of people. The smell of the food is overwhelming. My stomach is flipping. I just want to sit down and eat everything. Instead, I slide up to the bar, and lick my lips in anticipation of a cold drink.

I stand at the bar for a second before the bartender comes over. I'm the only one at the bar. Everyone else is seated at their tables ordering or eating one of the many courses they will enjoy tonight. "How can I help you, Sir?"

I'm dressed well, in slacks, a Coogi sweater, and a leather trench coat, but I'm disheveled. My hair is messed up with the leaves and small twigs sticking out of it. I wouldn't be surprised if I had insects crawling all over me after laying in that pile of leaves for all that time.

"I could use a ginger ale, a number for a cab and some change, please." I smile and look behind the bartender to the mirror that hung behind the bar, *I'm a mess.*

"Of course. Are you okay, Sir?" He asks, noticing my condition.

We lock eyes and I calmly say, "Yes, my car stalled out on the next block and I had to make my way here through the abandoned lot next to your restaurant. I took a tumble, but I'm fine. Thanks for asking."

He nodded and turned to get my drink.

"One more thing, please," I said before he got too far away.

"Yes, Sir, what is it?"

"Where's your bathroom?"

He pointed to a door off to the left. I nodded and made my way over to the door, pushed on it and was inside. I looked into the huge ornately framed mirror and saw just how disheveled I really looked. My hair was messed to the point of a rugby player, with leaves sticking out of it. Small twigs the size of toothpicks clung to my sweater along with grass and leaves alike. I stood there picking every last piece off of myself like a mother chimp picking at her baby chimp. I fixed my hair, washed my face, and straightened myself out as best I could. I walked out into the dining area and proceeded back to the bar.

The ten-dollar bill I had left for the drink and change was fanned out in a five-dollar bill and two singles, beside my glass of ginger ale, and a number written on a card. The bartender glanced at me from the end of the bar fifteen feet away. I nodded and thanked him. He nodded back. I picked up my drink and enjoyed the first drink I had since this had all started. I didn't realize how thirsty I was. I put the glass down as I noticed the small clock next to cash register, 7:47 p.m. It had been about three hours.

As hungry as I was, I just wanted to get home. I picked up the card with the taxi number written on it. *Seven digits is all I have to punch in and a car will be here to get me and take me home.* I walked out into the same foyer I came through and to the pay phone which swallowed up my quarter as I dial the number. I place the receiver to my ear, ring, ring, ring. "Taxi, how can I help you?"

"Yes, can I have a cab from the—" I flip the card over to see the name and address, "Cyprus Inn on 55 Baker Street, in Lakewood."

The voice says, "Fifteen minutes and that will be twenty-five dollars."

I respond, "That's fine. Tell the driver to beep, okay?"

"Yeah, you got it." The voice hangs up and so do I. And just as I turn to walk back into the restaurant, the shark pulls by the front door. I take another step and hear the brakes squeal. In my mind the shark has just bumped me. *Do I freeze or swim? I swim.*

As the cop car stops, I can hear the keys jingling behind me. I walk into the restaurant and as the front door opens, "Hey you. Hey!"

I'm in the restaurant scanning the room just as the Terminator would. *Two humans, male, male at first table, two male forms at next table. Four female humans at far table. Kitchen to the left, bathroom over to the right by the bar.* I step towards the kitchen as I hear the door open. From the foyer to the dining room, I hear, "Hey! Hold it!"

Credit Card at the Mall

I take off like a scared deer being startled by a hunter. I shoot past the first table then the second. I knock over a tray filled with food as I bump a waiter. There's only one way out. I pull my leather trench around me like Dracula preparing to turn into a bat. I run, and like the Cowardly Lion in *The Wizard of Oz,* I crash through the plate glass window of the restaurant.

I heard people yelling, cars beeping their horns from the roadway out front, and the voice of the cop as I try to stand up on the broken glass and run; him screaming at me to "freeze." The cop had drawn his gun and was pointing it right at me. A second cop car pulled up as this cop kept me covered. They arrested me and took me to jail.

I was charged with credit card fraud and destruction of property. Bail was set, I called a girlfriend, and went back to waiting. As I sat there and waited to get bailed out, I thought back to the day's events, standing at the locker taking the credit card, going into the mall, being chased, hiding, and *oh yeah, my car is still there with all the other stuff I got.* I smile slyly, then I frown.

Who was that guy in the gym, talking about God, and claiming that he was me? Maybe he called the cops on me? What was he saying again, something about labor, work? My thoughts are interrupted. "Paladino, you're out of here, let's go." I stand while the cop opens the cell. I walk out and get into my girlfriend's car and go get my car and go home.

A month later I showed up in court. They offered me three years. I went on the run and another crime spree until I was caught on December 20, 1991 for this and other charges.

SEASIDE HEIGHTS

It was a gorgeous summer day, the kind of day you spend all winter hoping for; not too hot and not too cool. I asked my girlfriend at the time, Tina, if she wanted to take a ride to Seaside Heights to enjoy a day on the boardwalk. She was in total agreement, so we started to get ready and called two other couples to see if they wanted to come with us, Ray and Margot, and Carl and Lacy. We designated a time for everyone to meet at our place, which was my grandparent's house in Lakewood.

They drove down from northern New Jersey and got to the house around 1 p.m. We all exchanged pleasantries and relaxed for an hour or so at the house. We had a simple plan, to drive to Seaside, walk the boards and have fun.

While we waited to leave, I had an idea that maybe I should bring my two dogs with us so they could have a nice day out also, and I could look cool walking two Pit bulls down the boardwalk. "Animal" and "Hawk" were aptly named after "The Road Warriors," a pro wrestling team I loved because of their brutal tactics and scary appearance.

Because of the dogs, we opted to take two cars, one with the guys and dogs, the other with our ladies. The ride to seaside from Lakewood only took thirty to forty minutes, during which, we caught up on guy talk, smoked some pot, and enjoyed some music. When we arrived, we found parking at an all-day lot close to the boardwalk and I walked the dogs to the back of the lot so they could pee. I couldn't help but smile to myself watching the girls primping themselves in the mirrors, one in the rearview, and one each at the side view mirrors. They all performed the same routine practically in unison.

The sun was shining. I could feel the warm rays hitting my face and arms. A light breeze was coming off the ocean, which was only across the street and up the wooden ramp. I could hear bells and whistles ringing and blowing. As we started to walk toward the boardwalk, the fragrance of cotton candy, pizza, funnel cake, Panama Jack suntan lotion and the sweet smell of the ocean all mingled together and filled the air. I always enjoyed the boardwalk more than just sitting on the beach all day.

We crossed the street at the corner and made our way up the ramp by the Castle Amusement Casino. The bells and whistles were loud along with balloons popping and the compressed air from the bb machine guns. I could hear a hundred sounds all at once as I walked up the ramp being pulled by the dogs on either side of me.

Once on the boards I gave Animal's leash to Tina, because he pulled less, and also so we could hold hands and walk side by side. To the left of the Midway, there was a sausage stand that smelled so good my mouth started to water immediately. The sausage frying on the grill and the peppers and onions were all I wanted at that moment, but we all decided to walk down a little bit, then stop back there on our way back.

Since it was the afternoon, the boardwalk wasn't crowded, but there were some people walking around pushing babies, playing games, eating, and looking at Animal and Hawk. Everybody wanted to pet them and the dogs loved it. They were two hams who loved the attention.

We walked towards the north end of the boardwalk toward the Sky Lift and the Aztec Bar. We stopped and played a couple of number games. The girls placed their bets on SAM, TED, PAM, DAD, MOM and STAR. Tina hit the button and the giant wheel with the matching names started to spin. The guy behind the counter was giving his spiel, "One winner, one winner, nobody knows where it stops, here we go." The wheel spun while a piece of plastic hit the metal pins sticking out from the round board. The sound reminded me of childhood memories from when we would put baseball cards with clothing pins on our bicycle wheels to make a similar sound. The wheel came to a slow stop. We all stood there staring at it, exalting our picks, *come on SAM, come on DAD, come on PAM*. And so, it went until it landed on SAM.

The guy yelled out over his microphone, we got a winner, winner, winner chicken dinner, it's SAM. Tina laughed and turned and said "I won, Boo." That was our cute little name for one another over the months we had been together. The guy came over and told her that she could pick anything on the middle shelf. She took a cute little teddy bear and we walked away as the guy started to sell his wares again. "Come on folks, we got a winner every time. Step right up and place your bets. There's a winner every time."

We walked down the boards, played a few more games, stopped at the sunglasses stand, bought some shades, and sat at the edge of the boardwalk for a while and surveilled the beach from our benches. We made our way back towards the other end in the same fashion, playing games, watching people, and letting kids pet the dogs.

We followed the aroma of the sausage, onions and peppers all the way to the Midway, where we stopped and ordered food, sausage sandwiches, fries, and sodas. Animal and Hawk even got a sandwich and a bowl of water. We lingered there for about thirty minutes, finished our food and walked further down toward Lucky Leo's. We played more games, won more prizes, and enjoyed our day in the sun to the fullest. We were laughing and joking all the way to the end of the boards, where we were headed so we could use the bathrooms and stop for some zeppoles and funnel cake before leaving.

We made it to the end of the boardwalk and stepped onto the blacktop of a huge parking lot that looked more like a marina. The blacktop looked like it was covered in dark murky water and all the cars looked like moored boats floating in the water with the sun sparkling off of the stainless-steel trimmings.

The bathrooms were in the last building at the end of the parking lot. The line wasn't too long, but long enough so that Ray and I left the girls with Carl so they could use the restrooms. I walked the dogs toward the far end of the parking lot.

Between us and the other end of the lot were about ten to twelve heavy metal type-dudes dressed in all black, leather vests, long black hair, black shades, black jeans, and heavy metal tee shirts representing various bands. Ray and I approached warily with Animal and Hawk leading the way, looking like we were in total contrast to these guys. We were dressed in pullover shirts and jean shorts, with our hair combed, and white spotless sneakers. Even our walk and attitude weren't of Seaside. We were definitely screaming north New Jersey without saying a word. We were about five feet away when the first words were spoken,

"Hey, what kind of dogs are they?" We were in the midst of them, basically surrounded.

I replied, "Pit bulls."

One of the heavy metal dudes says, "This one looks like a Pit bull, but the other one don't."

I say, "Well, he is. They're brothers from the same litter." They all just nod their heads.

"Where you guys from?" one of them asks.

So I say, "Lakewood" where my grandparent's house was, just to save us from a problem. It must have worked, because they asked if we wanted a beer. We agreed and took the beers and were sharing in the small talk when I look down and see Animal start to piss on one of the guy's legs. He notices it at the same moment and tries to kick Animal. I shove him backwards and hand the dogs off to Ray.

Some harsh words were exchanged, but finally calmer heads prevailed. A few tense moments went by and things seemed fine, until one of the heavy metal guys tries to pat his chest to get Animal to stand up on him. He doesn't know that that is the signal for Animal to jump up. And Animal, doing what I trained him to do, does just that. He jumped up at the guy and knocks his beer all over him.

I quickly say, "I'm sorry, dude." and pull Animal away. I guess my sorry seemed insincere to him, because he flicked his beer-soaked fingers at me and sprayed me with beer. My first inclination was to knock him out, but seeing how we were outnumbered twelve to two, and I had the dogs with me, I wiped it off and tried to make a joke out of it. But my mind started to plan how I could get this guy.

I gave Ray the dogs and told him to get the girls and Carl and head for our cars. He knew I was going to knock out as many as I could and run to the cars, but as he walked away, I noticed the guy who flicked me with beer sitting and toweling himself off near the coolers with the beer. Then I noticed him pull out a big bag of pot and get ready to roll a joint, so I quickly say, "Hey man, I'm really sorry for that. Hey, do you want to sell me a joint for $5?"

He turns and can't resist the $5 bill I had pulled out. "Yeah, I'll sell you a joint, he says with a smile."

I tell him, "Let's go by the bench so no cops can see us." He agrees. We walk away from the main group and head to the ramp leading to the bench. I already know in my head I'm going to rob him for his stash. We walk down the ramp.

I can feel my 260-pound frame shift forward. We hit the platform at the bottom. He pulls out the bag of pot, and some rolling papers, and hands me the pot to hold and open the bag while he takes out the amount he plans to roll for the joint he is going to sell me. It's then that I hear my name, "John."

I turn expecting to see Ray, but instead see somebody is walking down the ramp toward me, but I can't see his face because I'm looking into the sun. "Yo, I thought I told you to take the dogs and go get the—"

Then I see a man who looks just like me, only a little older and bald. "John, listen to me, you're about to make a huge mistake."

I reply, "No, you listen. You better get out of here before *you* make a huge mistake."

I turn so my back isn't to the heavy metal dude, and I see he is frozen in time. I turn back to the sound of the man's voice once more, "John, you're not going to understand this, but I'm you coming to warn you that you're going to make a huge mistake and to let you know you have a choice to do right instead."

"Who are you? Me? What are you taking about? Get out of my way." I try to walk up the ramp but can't move.

"John, God loves you and wants to see you do right. He has plans for you, John. All you have to do is make the right decision. Listen to His Word in Zachariah 11:3... 'There is the sound of wailing shepherds! For their glory is the ruins. There is the sound of roaring lions! For the pride of the Jordan is in ruins.'"

I turn back to the heavy metal dude, then back to the guy on the ramp. "Listen, man—" he's gone.

The heavy metal guy says "Hey man, give me my bag." I roll it up and put it in my pocket and walk up the ramp. The heavy metal guy starts to follow me. I turn and tell him back off.

He replies, "Give me my dope, man."

I get up the ramp and start to walk across the black sea of tar toward the street away from this guy and his heavy metal crew of pirates. He's following me and yelling across the parking lot to his friends for help. I turn again and tell him to "get the F away from me." He continues to yell to his friends and walk towards me. I step back, breaking my stride, and wait for him to walk up to me. I see his friends now notice the commotion and are walking towards us from the other side. He yells some profanities at me and comes at me to attack me. I punch him as hard as I can in the face and he hits his head on a car bumper and crashes to the ground. His friends take off running toward me.

I start to walk away quickly to the corner of a building, with the intention of turning the corner and running. I looked back and to see them stop at their friend, the one I knocked out. I looked at them, they looked at me, and start running toward me. I turned to walk around the corner and right as I step around the corner, I walk right into a cop who was coming around the corner towards me at the exact same time.

"Whoa, fella, slow down," the cop says.

My mouth opens and out comes, "Officer, these guys are trying to jump me." Just as the words come out, the whole group of heavy metal dudes comes running up and stops, not knowing what to say.

The cop says, "What's going on here?" They say that I punched their friend. I say they tried to harass me, my friends and our girls.

They looked like a bunch of scum bags and we all looked nice and clean cut. Ray, Carl and the girls walked up just as all of this was happening. The cop asks for my ID. I give it to him and he lets us go, while he stops the heavy metal guys from following.

We got to our cars and drove home to my grandparents' house in Lakewood and partied and chilled the weekend away.

About a month later I got a summons to appear in court for aggravated assault and robbery. The guy said I robbed him for $200, and he was suing me for hospital bills because I broke his whole eye socket. This happened around the same time as the credit card shopping spree and some other problems I had with the law, so that's when I went on the run for about two years.

I was all over the place, mentally and physically. A close friend of mine, "Big O" and I, partnered in many endeavors. We took what we wanted, said what we wanted, and acted how we wanted, and if you didn't like it, we'd beat you how we wanted.

I loved to party, fight and be amorous. I had always considered myself a ladies' man and had always been lucky in love. I spent my time ripping it up, fueled with alcohol, drugs, and violence. I haven't even documented the number of fights, thefts, and violent acts that occurred during these years. I was a runaway train headed for a huge pileup. I never once had any thoughts of doing anything legit. I worked, but with the thought in my head of what could I steal, and how could I use the job to benefit myself on the side beyond my paycheck.

While I was on the run in Florida, I had run into an old buddy of mine, who I did some time with at Yardville as a youth. We joined forces and burgled the pawn shops. We robbed guns, jewelry, anything of value and we were good at it. We'd rob one pawn shop only to pawn the stuff in another one.

When things got hot, I got a job on a fishing boat long lining. What an experience that was, fourteen days at sea for a kid from north New Jersey who only ever went waist deep in the ocean. But it was how I lived life; everything was an adventure.

When I did finally get caught, the judge gave me thirty days for disorderly conduct, running together with the three flat that I got for the credit card situation.

GOGO BAR ASSAULT

One night in August, I was at Century Field in Garfield with Tina. I was practicing flag football and she was sitting on the side along with a few other girlfriends of some of the guys on the team as well.

It was hot; we were all dripping with sweat and tired, so we ended the practice early. The real reason though, was that Tina's cousin was having his bachelor party that night and we were all going, even though our girls were all making a big stink about it. We tried to downplay the fact that it was at a go-go bar named AJ's in Jersey City, but it did little to help our cause. All the girls were irritated with us. Even Tina, who was normally pretty cool about such things, was asking me not to go. She said she had a feeling "something bad was going to happen," as we walked to our car.

I was carrying her beach chair and the small cooler we had with water and ice. She had her purse and my arm as we walked across the grass to the parking lot to the car. I opened the trunk, put the chair and the cooler in, and sat on the edge of the open trunk, pulled her to me and kissed her on the lips and said, "Don't worry, nothing is gonna happen, I promise. I'll even come home early, okay?"

She wasn't convinced in the least. She persisted some more, but by the time we got home, she had dropped it and was giving me the cold shoulder, and a bit of the silent treatment. I showered, shaved, threw on my favorite Sergio Tacchini sweat suit, my favorite gold chain, and my new sneakers. I heard the horn outside, looked at Tina on the couch ignoring me, and thought for a half of a second about not going just to avoid a fight.

Instead, I said, "I love you Boo" and leaned down and kissed her. She didn't return the kiss. I walked out and slammed the door shut, thinking to myself, *Now I'm definitely not coming home early.*

I stepped out into the hot summer air. I could hear the club music coming from my friend Ray's Cadillac. He was sitting in the car with the air blasting and bopping his head back and forth to the music as he preened himself vainly in the rearview mirror. I walked around to the passenger side, pulled open the door and hopped in.

The club music came alive with treble and bass pumping. We looked at each other and nodded as we gave each other a fist pound (a handshake with fists bumping into each other, knuckles first). No words were exchanged. He threw the car into drive and pulled away. I looked over at my house and could see Tina staring out of the front window. I turned my head and didn't look back.

We pulled down the block, made a left and stopped to pick up Jason. He was waiting in front of his mother's house smoking a cigarette. Ray pulled over, I opened the door and Jason climbed in. He yelled over the music, "What's up." It was more of a greeting than a question. We drove through town to the highway. My beeper buzzed in my pocket. I checked it and smiled. The digits 143 were on the small narrow screen. It was from Tina and it was our code for "I love you."

We raced down the highway in anticipation of a great night. We all agreed to meet at the place at nine. We pulled in and saw some of the guys standing there, laughing and joking by their cars. We parked, stepped out onto the heavy gravel lot and walked over by the guys.

Just as we were talking Mike (Tina's cousin), Shorty (Mike's brother) and our friend Dave pulled into the lot. The gravel crunched beneath the tires as they drove past us all smiling from ear to ear. The muffled sound of Frank Sinatra's "Summer Wind" faded as they drove by and parked, then it came in loud and clear as the passenger door opened, but it died when the car was immediately turned off.

We all exchanged congrats, hugs, handshakes, and kisses on the cheeks and then we moved across the parking lot in unison like a pack of hungry wolves. We were ten in all from our neighborhood, but Mike had other friends of his from work coming too, but they were told 9:30 so we could get the room we rented in order and get the lay of the land.

You could hear the music from inside pumping. The door opened, and two young guys stumbled out smiling and laughing. The music and voices were louder now. "Yo, the girls are hot, man," one of the two guys said.

We all just laughed and nodded as we filtered into the place. It was dark except for the flashing lights around the stage. The smell of beer and spilled drinks hit us immediately. Guys were yelling, music was blasting, and the girls were gyrating. A big bouncer stepped out of the shadows, "There's a cover guys, five dollars, plus I got to see ID." Shorty, Mike's brother, had made all the reservations, so he started talking to the bouncer. I couldn't hear what was said, but the guy nodded and walked toward the inner sanction.

He stopped and waved somebody over. Some guy, who looked like a weasel, came into view, walked over, shook hands with Shorty and Mike, and nodded for us to follow behind. Like a bunch of kids on a school trip we filled in behind the weasel. He walked us down a short hallway, past a door that was open where I spotted a beautiful blond standing in front of a mirror putting lipstick on. She saw me and blew a kiss at me in the mirror. I smiled and moved on.

At the end of the hall was a door. He opened it and walked in, we all followed. Once inside it was easier to hear the weasel, who had apparently been talking the whole time. "Shut the door," the weasel said. Somebody behind me shut it. The outside sound was dimmed, but by no means deadened.

"Okay, guys, welcome to AJ's. This is your private room with a fully loaded bar and bartender. That's Jack, guys. He's good. Over there is your buffet. Plates, forks, napkins are all on the tables. Two girls will be here shortly. Any questions? Oh yeah, you're not locked in here. You're free to visit the main bars. That's your call, okay? Then I'll check on you guys later. For now get comfortable, have some drinks, and enjoy."

And just like that he left without a word. Most of us went to the bar and started ordering drinks and beers. A few of us went to see what the food looked like.

There was a long table filled with four-inch pans loaded with wings, sausage and peppers, pasta, salad, tons of bread, and rolls. It was a feast with plenty to go around. A couple of the guys started to dig in right away.

I went to the bar first to wet my whistle. "Give me a Jack and Coke, Jack." He looked at me and thought twice about sending a wise crack back. "I got ya" was all he said. As he turned to grab the bottle of Jack Daniels, I saw Mike standing there with a beer. "Congrats, Bro, I wish you nothing but love and happiness," I said. We made some small talk. A few of us ordered shots and toasted Mike several times.

It quickly turned into a sort of a roast. We were telling stories, drinking and greeting the guys from his job and other friends. The night was moving on. We told Dave to go and tell the weasel we were ready for the girls. He came back and said it would be about thirty minutes or so. It was hitting 10:00 already, and a few of the guys and myself were getting antsy. We decided to go out to the main bar. We talked Mike and Mini into coming also.

We went out into the dimly lit bar and the music was so loud your body felt like it was vibrating. We made our way through the crowd up to the bar. We all started cashing in fifties and hundreds for singles. We shoved money into Mike's hands and told him to go to town.

We waved over some girls who quickly upon seeing all the singles came swaying and sashaying over. Mike was smiling and handing out dollar bills left and right. We just stood by and watched.

After a few minutes I drifted away and started to walk around the bar to look at the sights. I was in a jovial mood, feeling good and enjoying myself, when suddenly, some guy bumps into me and knocks my drink all over me. He looks at me with a nasty look and says, "Watch it man."

Now, in my head I know he doesn't know who I am or what I'm capable of. Usually, I would have beat this guy up on the spot, got tossed out, and went somewhere else, but tonight was different. I didn't want to ruin Mike's or anyone else's good time, so I smiled and said, "Sorry my bad, and walked away." I heard the guy grumble something as he walked away.

I walked to the other end of the bar sipping on what was left of my drink. This place was huge. It had two square bars with stages in the middle and about a hundred stools around each. I walked slowly to the other side thinking nothing of the guy that bumped into me, as I was watching the show the girls were putting on. In my mind, I was calculating how much each of the girls was making. And then, bam. I get knocked into again.

I say to myself, *it can't be*, but it was. It was the same guy. He gave me a look as if to say, *what are you going to do about it?* I couldn't believe it was happening, my temper was starting to flare. I caught myself and said "My bad" again, with a hint of sarcasm in my tone. It hardly mattered, he probably couldn't even hear me. He shot me a dirty look, and I walked away shaking my head. I walked to the opposite bar, ordered a drink, left the change, and backed away from the three-deep-crowd at the bar.

I saw Mike and guys on the other side and decided to make my way over to see how they were doing. I made it to the corner of the bar. They were at the opposite corner hooting and hollering. I took the first of the forty or so steps that would place me by their side and bam, I get bumped from the side. I look and sure enough, it's the same guy.

He's targeted me again, for whatever his reason was, I realized that this guy was deliberately trying to start a fight with me. "Hey, watch it," he vehemently says.

I've had enough. I snap, "No, you ******* watch it. What's up with you?"

We start to argue, right in each other's faces. I drop my drink and I am just about to smash him in his face when the big bouncer from the door steps between us and says, "Is there a problem?"

"No, I'm just here wanting a good time. This guy wants trouble."

The guy becomes belligerent, starts threatening me, and coming at me. The bouncer pushes him back and with a word he calms him, "Yo, chill man." The guy backs down but is shooting daggers at me from his eyes. I stand there calmly as the big bouncer continues, "Ain't you with the bachelor party in the back?"

"Yeah," I reply.

"Okay, why don't you go back to your party and I'll take care of this."

I nod and walk past the big bouncer and over to the guys, "What's up? You guys good?" I ask. They say "Yeah, we're headed to the back."

We all head back to the private room. Not even five minutes goes by and a girl comes in and everybody starts to go crazy whistling and yelling. Shorty and I quickly make a circle with the chairs and place one in the middle. Somebody brings Mike to the middle chair and everybody starts to sit in the chairs around the circle.

Me and Shorty go to the bar and tell Jack to give us two trays of shots for everybody so we can toast Mark in unison. He pours out thirty shots, fifteen on each tray. We walk over and pass them out.

The girl is dancing in the center of the circle and as she starts her routine with Mike, we all stand up with our shots and close the circle in tight. We hold our shots up high, like knights of the round table minus the swords. We all yell, then you hear someone scream the four words that would bring the party to a halt, a screeching halt, "Pour it on him!"

So, in our buzzed states of mind, instead of downing shots we dump our shots over Mike and the go-go girl. Thirty shots simultaneously pour out, each a mini waterfall. We're all smiles as the liquor hits her and then Mike. He doesn't seem to care, but the girl jumps up covered in liquor, her hair matted down to her face and her expression contorts into a combination of utter disbelief and anger.

"What the ****" she curses. "Are you crazy? I got to finish working!" she's screaming and flipping out, (and in hindsight, rightly so). She grabs her bag and storms out.

We all break out laughing and joking and somebody says "When do the other girls get here?"

An answer comes, "Any time, now."

I say to Dave, "Whatever, at least we didn't pay her."

Then I see the look on his face, "We gave her $200 by the bar."

"What," I say in disbelief. *We paid her to come back.* I start to calculate the time and money. She was only back here for ten minutes. "Go get your money back, at least 150, a buck-fifty." So, we decide that me, Dave, Shorty, and Jason are going to go to the front, talk to the weasel and get at least some of the money back, if not all. After all, what's fair is fair. That girl hardly put on a show and walked out with $200 for ten minutes.

So, there we were, walking down that door-filled hallway, the only brightly lit place in the whole building. It seemed so surreal being in that short tunnel walking towards the dark outer rooms. *Wasn't it supposed to be the other way around, from darkness into the light?*

I looked back at the now closed door and I felt as though I had no choice but to continue marching forward to what I thought would be an easy task; to explain to the weasel what happened, get the money, tell him to send back the other girls, continue to party and have a great night. I was wrong. As we shuffled out of the tunnel, we found ourselves paused for a moment. Each one of us was looking in a different direction. We were scanning the floor for the weasel.

Between concentrating on the task at hand and watching the girls on stage it was hard to focus for a moment. Then I saw him standing at the far end of the main bar stage area by a back wall talking to some patron. "I see him," I said to no one in particular, and started to walk towards him. When suddenly out of the corner of my eye I spot the guy who kept bumping me. Our eyes met and my mind starts racing, thinking to myself, *I thought the bouncer would have thrown him out.*

I noticed the guy pick up his beer bottle by the neck, his obvious intention wasn't to drink the beer but to use the bottle as a weapon. He had grabbed the bottle thumb down around the neck instead of thumb up. I thought to myself, *even with the bottle he doesn't stand a chance.* I looked over my shoulder and told my friends, "Wait here. I'll go talk to the weasel, be right back."

They really had no clue about what I knew was going to happen. I stepped forward pretending not to see the bumper standing there with bottle in hand. "John," a voice said clearly, somehow it sounded like a whisper in my head and it drowned out the loud blaring music. I turned, thinking it was one of my friends, but they were standing about fifteen feet away and intently concentrating on the stage show.

Then from the side wall someone stepped forward. I almost raised my arm in a defensive fashion thinking somehow the "bumper" had gotten on the other side of me. "John, listen to me for a minute," everything seemed to stand still except for this guy and me. I thought for a second it had to be one of the bumper's boys trying to sneak me from the side. I instinctively said "Yo, my man, back up."

His reply confused me, because I couldn't comprehend how he knew my name. "John, listen to me, this won't make sense to you, but I'm you trying to..."

I snapped back, "What the **** are you saying? I'm telling you man, back up or else." I braced myself for the attack I thought was coming, but instead I noticed something familiar about this guy, something in his eyes, something beneath his heavily tattooed arm, something familiar about the gray goatee that once was black came over me as I listened.

"John, I know you can't understand this right now, but you're about to make a big mistake even though it isn't your fault. You can walk away before you hurt someone really badly."

I furiously snap back, "I didn't start this, your boy did and if he doesn't back down, he's gonna get hurt."

The big bald headed tatted older guy spoke in a calm tone. "John, I am you and I'm here to warn you about what's gonna happen. Please listen to me. God loves you and has a plan for you, but you must make the right choice tonight. Listen to what God says in Ephesians 4:26, 'Be angry and do not sin. Do not let the sun go down on your wrath, nor give place to the devil.'"

I heard laughing and shouting behind me. I turned to see what it was, all the guys at the bar were watching a girl on the stage. I turned back to the stranger who said he was me, but found no one standing there. I looked right, then left, nothing. The stranger was gone.

The only familiar face I saw was the "bumper" staring at me with fire in his eyes, which threw the switch in my brain back into warrior mode. Before I could register a strategy, I stepped forward toward the weasel. He stood at the end of this narrow width of walkway between the bar and wall. From my peripheral view I saw the bumper to my left. One more step and we would be side by side.

My foot landed, I braced for the impact of the bottle. My foot lifted and I landed one step further away from the bumper and closer to the weasel. I kept my defenses up, thinking he was going to attack from behind, but I didn't care. I was too cocky, too big, and too psyched up to even care. Another step landed, nothing.

I made it to the weasel in two more steps and explained our situation. He reached in his pocket, pulled, out two $100 bills and handed them to me. "Here you go, I'll straighten it out with her later. Go enjoy your party, the girls will be back in about ten minutes." He smiled at me with his little weasel teeth. I said thanks, and walked away.

My attention shifted and my thoughts, and every tense muscle now were focused on the "bumper." This time I didn't advert my gaze, I stared right at him, daring him with my eyes to do something. Step by step, I grew closer to this coward with the bottle still clenched in his hand. As I stepped forward, one more length of my legs would put me within arm's reach of him.

We stared at one another like two gunslingers poised to draw at any second. We each waited for the other to make the first move. Another step and I was a foot away, when suddenly, he swung with the bottle. I didn't even try to block it, instead I fired off a right and left. My punch landed right on target. The bottle hit my head and smashed into pieces as he fell back from my forceful hits. The only thing that kept him up was the guy he fell into at the bar.

I fired off another round of powerful punches, tagging him again and again. Within a second, a huge fight broke out with me on one side, my friends on the other side, and people just letting loose. It was mayhem. I swung at whatever or whoever was in front of me.

People fell under the heavy barrage of blows I threw. I took a few random hits, but nothing to deter my animal instinct of kill or be killed. I threw well-placed shots, until after what felt like long minutes, but were probably only short seconds, the bouncers came running over pulling people apart. The music cut off, the lights were put on and flooded every inch of darkness.

Four bouncers had me pinned against the back wall. I was struggling against them to no avail. They were facing me, telling me to calm down while I stared out toward the sea of bodies and carnage. I saw the "bumper" come out of nowhere with hate in his eyes, blood in his mouth, and blood flowing from his nose.

He ran up while I was helpless and vulnerable. I reflectively turned my head to try to deflect the blow I thought he was going to cowardly throw, but instead I felt a tug at my neck as he reached in and snatched my chain off my neck, my favorite solid gold rope chain with my diamond cut ornate cross.

I looked at him as he smirked and ran away. My eyes watched as he jetted to the side door. I struggled more intensely, only to be met with stronger resistance from the bouncers. Seconds were ticking away as the "bumper" made his getaway.

"Okay, okay, I'm calm, let me go, let me go." I pleaded as they lessened their hold on me. I broke free and ran toward the door the "bumper" had escaped through. I hit the door hard at full speed. It flew open, smashed against the outside of the building. I thought the "bumper" was long gone, but to my utter surprise and astonishment there he was, right in front of me with two friends holding up my chain as his trophy.

I ran straight at them. They didn't even have time to react as I punched the first guy so hard, I knocked him out of his shoes. The second guy took off running, while the "bumper" tried to attack me from behind, only to be met by Dave, who had just come through the door. Dave grabbed him and was bear hugging him as I turned to face them, "Let him go!" I yelled. Dave released him.

He stepped forward as if to fight. I punched him so hard that he flew backwards and hit his head against the building and went down hard. I ran up to him and started to stomp him over and over until he was lifeless on the ground. Even then I continued to kick him and stomp on his face until finally Dave pulled me off of him. I was in a rage and probably would have killed him, if Dave hadn't pulled me away.

I left him where he laid, but not before riffling his pockets, getting my chain and what cash I found. We went back inside, made our way to our reserved party room, where I proceeded to flip out, and flip the food table, accusing my friends of not having my back.

I finally calmed down, went to the bar and had a few drinks. Within twenty minutes I was called out to the front along with Dave and Jason. The cops wanted to question us about the half dead guy who was hanging on by a thread.

First, they checked our hands. When we all played dumb the cop gave a long speech about how this guy might die, then he'd see who had nothing to say. He pointed Dave and me out of the crowd of us and said somebody told us you two were out here fighting, give me some ID. Dave pulled out his wallet, handed his license over to the cop, who wrote down his info.

I said I don't have any ID on me. The cop asked me my info, which I relayed falsely to him. I gave him an alias and wrong address. "We'll be in touch with you two if this guy doesn't make it." I found Ray and him and I got out of there and went back home, where I had to listen to Tina give me the "I told you so" speech.

A few days went by when I got beeped to call a number. It was a good friend of mine, Jeff. He told me that the cops had called Dave and told him if he didn't give me up, he was going to have to take the blame for what happened to the "bumper." Apparently, the "bumper" was in the hospital in bad shape, and somebody had to pay.

Dave must have figured it wasn't going to be him, so he told Jeff that he wasn't going to take the blame for me and instead he was going to go to Italy for a month. The next thing I knew, the cops had my name, address, date of birth, social security number, everything, and they put out a warrant for me; which was one of many others at the time. Needless to say, I was now wanted for the assault. It wasn't long before I had a run in with the cops.

I got arrested and was charged with aggravated assault. The "bumper" was so badly beaten that he lost nine teeth, had cranial damage, facial damage and now had the capacity of a ten-year-old. At least that's what he claimed in his lawsuit. Since this happened right around the time of the credit card thing and the Seaside Heights thing my lawyer worked out a deal to have everything run together into one sentence. I got a three flat and was sent to Southern State Prison in New Jersey.

SECOND TIME IN PRISON: SOUTHERN STATE

Much like my first time in prison, my second time was even a bigger joke. I had just come back to New Jersey from being on the run in Florida. I only came back because my girlfriend, Tina, was pregnant with my first child.

When I got back, I tried to keep a low profile, but staying under the radar was proving harder than it seemed for me, especially because I loved the limelight, loved partying, and loved the ladies. So, it wasn't long before my name started to get kicked around town and it especially didn't help that I was collecting monies and using unsavory tactics to do so. It was on one such occasion when I was out collecting that the cops mysteriously showed up in full force. They came with a small army and rightly so. To be modest, I must admit, I was a problem, so I guess they figured they had better be prepared to handle me. I escaped their clutches through a back door and hid in an overgrown grass-filled yard.

I laid there and smoked a joint, while staring up at the stars thinking of only one thing the whole time, getting home to my apartment to say goodbye to Tina, who was a couple of weeks short of giving birth. It was December 20th.

I got up, made my way to an ally, navigated my way through a bevy of cops until finally one of them inquisitively asked another cop standing there, "Where did that guy come out of?" They called me over, but instead I took off running. As I looked back over my shoulder cops were filtering out of every crevice on that block. And since the neighborhood was on a hill it looked like ants crawling down off an ant hill to attack an intruder.

I ran, they followed. Finally, as I got tired, I was headed off by a cop car on a set of railroad tracks. The pursuing hoard of cops crashed into and onto me while we all crashed into the side of the cop car. They proceeded to slam me, but there were too many of them to get any real damaging blows landed. They were like a horde of hyenas on a lone lion.

Finally, they parted and allowed one of their trained dogs to attack me on his own merit. He was a big German shepherd who was trained to take down ordinary people. He jumped at me, mouth open, baring his teeth. Instead of pulling back, I shoved my forearm so far down his throat and held the back of his head that it became apparent very quickly that it was a losing battle for him. I threw him into the air, where he landed on all fours, but before he could resume his attack he was pulled away by another cop and I was forced into the back of the cop car.

I was processed and sent to the county (Bergen). From there, after a short stay, to Hudson. From Hudson, I was sent to a tent unit in south New Jersey, where I quickly became acquainted with the officers by way of taking a tent hostage, which landed me roughly in the hole in Leesburg State Prison. After a 30 day stay, I was unfortunately processed back through the tents, which sat between two state prisons, Leesburg and Southern State.

After another (this time) uneventful stay in the tents I was moved to Southern State Prison to finish my time. When I made it onto the main compound, I thought I was on a college campus. There was a huge track that circled around the whole compound, with walkways crossing through the center, heading off to different trails or units placed around the entire prison compound.

Flowers were planted row after row and in small patches throughout the area, and beautifully manicured green grass covered the ground where track or flowers hadn't been planted. Cement benches dotted the walkways for weary travelers. It wasn't what I expected at all.

There were six trailer units on this compound. This was phase I of II. Phase II was phase I's twin. I was processed in at unit one, orientation, that took thirty days. I was moved to unit four, where I reported, and was assigned to F tier, bed twelve. It was a top bunk at the end of the small tier.

As soon as you walked into the unit there was an open area, where an officer sat behind a desk. Beyond him was an open kitchen area. To the left were two separate dayrooms with picnic-type tables and benches and a TV in each room. The first room was the sports room, only sports were watched on this TV. The second area and slightly larger was the common area. This room and TV were used for movies and general TV watching, plus there were two microwaves on the counters in the corner to cook with.

Outside this area is where the small tiers were located, which each held twelve guys. So, every unit, which was a beehive of tiers, had 120 guys in them. At the front of each tier was the bathroom, which had a sink and mirror, a toilet area, and a shower. Three guys could be in there at once, but that was hardly ever the case, unless it was an emergency. Everybody respected each other's private time for the most part. After all, in a tier atmosphere, the bathroom was the only place you could get any private time.

The tier was set up as follows: A bunk bed, then about three feet away a single bed, then a small four-foot-high dividing wall, a single bed, the three-foot separation, then bunk bed, then a full wall. And on the other side, bunk bed, single four-foot dividing wall, single three-foot area, then bunk bed. Each man had a wall locker and footlocker at the head and foot of their beds.

Each unit, one through six, on the compound was enclosed by its own separate fence. It was its own smaller prison inside the larger prison compound. In case of riots the prison could be cut off into separate sections, which made it easier to control. In the morning, when the gates to the units were opened up to the main compound it was a beehive of activity. People would make their way to the gym, school, library, work, medical unit, yard or just out to walk around the main compound track.

We were allowed to come and go from the compound and gym building back to our units during this time. The only time we had to mandatorily (sic) be in the unit and on our tiers by our beds was during count time, which occurred several times a day, especially at shift change.

My stay in Southern State wasn't bad for the most part. We were allowed our own clothes, fifty pounds of food from home per month, and we were allowed to work out all day every day. Visits on the weekends were in the gym and pretty loose for the most part.

By now Jackie, my daughter, had been born and Tina was bringing her to see me every once in a while. She had gotten married and would sneak down to see me almost every weekend, most times alone. I spent my days working out, lifting, playing handball, and walking the track.

At night I'd read and write letters, or I could be found working at my new hobby, writing books for Jackie, with her as the main character.

Incidents were few. I only had to knock out two people, one a guy who stole my batteries out of my Walkman in the middle of the night, which I caught him doing red-handed, and another guy who thought he was a match for me. It was his ego and pride that sunk his ship.

The other incident was when someone's bed area was intentionally set on fire, but that's a story for another time. I got out in the beginning of 1994, ready to start my life over, fresh and clean at twenty-seven years old. It didn't go that way at all.

SMELL OF BLOOD

I started a small construction company, did some masonry work and dabbled in some collections, drugs, and gambling. I got myself a basement apartment in Lodi, New Jersey. Tina and I had this love-hate relationship, so she would come over to my place and we'd spend time together. Other than that quality time, we fought. She was married to someone else by the time I got out, but it never stopped us from being together physically.

I spent almost every weekend with Jackie and loved every minute of it. Then, after only a few months out, I had a bad motorcycle accident and busted up my left leg really bad, almost to the point of having it amputated. It took almost two years before I was back up and around. After all that down time, I hit the streets running again. I was far behind in earnings, so I stepped it up with the collecting and selling.

I started to get back on track, then I busted up my hand while busting up some guy from another crew who felt he didn't have to pay me. I was so good at collecting that my reputation grew and with it, fear. People would rather pay than have to deal with me. I got involved with a guy who was, (unbeknownst to me or the guy I was around), using our names to shake down an old partner of his, in the massage business.

Well, once I found out, sheerly by chance, I plotted to kill him. While all this was going on, the Feds were watching us and my friend's HMO company. At this point we were driving around in limos and SLE 500 Mercedes convertibles Town Cars and living it up. We had legit and illegit stuff going on and it was my job to make sure it all ran nice and smoothly in both worlds.

Not many people know that large amounts of blood pooled up, splattered or smeared on clothes or the floor, has the distinct smell of copper, just like a hand full of pennies held up to your nose. As an enforcer, a collector, and the muscle for a crew of guys, my main job was to instill fear, both mentally and physically into people who refused, couldn't pay, or had an excuse not to pay on debts—or if they had in some fashion disrespected a member of the crew. In this life, you never said no unless you wanted to be the recipient of a bullet to the back of your head, or worse, an outcast from the life. As Machiavelli once said, "Which would you prefer, to be loved or feared?" I always chose feared. It made things so much easier for me to carry out my job description, which was to get results, and to get the money at all costs. I was trained in the things that smelled like blood. I had become a professional in my field. My collection routine exemplified this thinking.

"You got the money?" I'd ask as I approached the unsuspecting debtor.

"I think the office made a mistake with my bets," he replied.

"Oh yeah? Well, listen and listen closely. I'm going to call the office and listen to the tapes and if you're lying..." I say these words with venom in my voice. "I hate getting the run around, but proper mob etiquette requires me to make sure before I send somebody to the hospital."

Mikey replies in a worried small voice, "You know I wouldn't lie to you. I'm telling you they made a mistake. I only put in a four timer on the Jets."

And in a disgruntled voice I say, "I don't give a ****. I just want the money if you owe it."

"Okay, okay, just call, you'll see," he stammers.

"I'll see you tomorrow right here at 3:00 to straighten this out, got it?"

He leaves. I go into the office of my little hand car wash and detail shop, make a few calls and leave so I can meet a few more people and use a pay phone. I hated phones. I'd seen too many guys get busted by talking on the phone about things they should never have been talking about. I even took the phone out of my apartment for a while just so I wouldn't become lazy one day and make that mistake myself.

The next day comes, and Mikey doesn't show. Now I'm pissed off. I beep him and he doesn't call back. I beep again, no call back. Now I'm in my office fuming. I'm so mad that I notice my knuckles are white as I squeeze the phone and dial his beeper with my number, nothing. I go out, do my regular routine, meet people, collect money, take bets, and make my presence known in the streets. I know it's only a matter of time before I bump heads with this guy and then I'll make an example of him, just like some others in the past.

All I keep telling myself is, *you're only as feared as the last person you put in the hospital.* Fear makes my job so much easier. A few days goes by, and Mikey is ducking my calls and avoiding me like the plague. *All this, over three grand.* Gamblers were worse than drug addicts, they were always trying to get one over. They always thought they knew the winner, and when they didn't win, they tried to catch up by placing more bets, thinking they'd cover their losses. But all they did was bury themselves in more debt and bring the wrath of me down on themselves when they couldn't pay. It was a vicious cycle that they never won. "The house always wins," at least that's what an old timer told me years ago. He might have been making a joke; after all his name was "Jimmy the House."

The office told me that the tapes were correct, and he was lying, but I didn't need them to tell me that; Mikey admitted his guilt by not showing the next day. I wasn't mad anymore, now it was just business. And in order for business to run smoothly there had to be order, and in order for there to be order, Mikey had to pay and go to the hospital, and not in that order.

Finally, three days later he called. I picked up the phone, "Yeah. Hey, it's me. I'm sorry I didn't meet you Tuesday or return your call I was out of—"

"Where are you now? Come to the car wash."

"I -- I -- I'm in New York. I won't be back until Monday."

"Okay, call me Monday." I hang up, plotting his demise. Nobody makes me look bad.

Saturday afternoon I have a flunky of mine beep Mikey, because I heard he was around town. The guy went and used the pay phone across the street at the auto parts store. Mikey called him right back. I had already told my guy to lure him there to the car wash by telling him I wasn't around and to bring the money or whatever he had to keep the peace because I had talked to the office.

Mikey reluctantly agreed. I pulled my car down the block and waited in my office. Finally, after waiting all week, I'd have my revenge. I waited patiently in my office watching out of the two-way glass. Thirty minutes later, Mikey walks in acting as if nothing were wrong, shaking hands with my guy and smiling up a storm.

I walked out of my office, still in my Mark Anthony Butter leather jacket. I've always heard of people turning white in the face of fear, but this time I really witnessed it, and I did so with pleasure. "You bring the money?" was all I said.

He replied, "I have some of—" and time seemed to stop.

As Mikey and my guy stood in front of me frozen, I looked around and standing in my office doorway was a guy that looked like me. I shook my head and did a double take for a minute. I thought I was looking into the full-length mirror I had against the wall, but that was in the back of the office. Then the mouth on the guy opened. I just stood there in shock.... "John, it's okay, I'm you. You won't understand this, but just relax for a minute. I have to tell you something, so please listen closely."

"Whoa, whoa, whoa, what is this? What's going on? What is this, a joke?" I looked at Mikey and my guy, but they were just standing as still as marble statues.

"No John, this is no joke. This is a matter of life and death seriousness. I know what you're about to do, John, and I also know that you have a choice between right and wrong. The choice you make will determine what your future will be like for the next ten years."

"What are you talking about ten years, choices? What is this nonsense?"

"John, listen to me and know this, God loves you and wants to see you do good. He has a plan for you, John, and your life. Listen to His word in Ephesians 4:26-27 ... He says, 'Be angry and do not sin. Do not let the sun go down on your wrath, nor give place to the devil.' Remember, this, John?"

"Listen, if you're here trying to get this lying piece of garbage out of this, then you better put $3,000 on the table and leave." I hear a noise behind me and turn but turn back just as fast. The guy in my office doorway isn't there. I step closer to my office doorway and peer in, it's empty except for my image in the mirror looking back at me.

Mikey's words startle me a little as his sentence carries on, "... it, not all, but I'll get the rest. Just give me a day or—" his words are cut short as I spin around, take two quick steps in his direction and punch him as hard as I possibly can in the jaw with a right hook. His jaw and head both rip sideways and slam into whatever muscle in his neck put on the brakes. If not for that muscle, his head might have spun around twenty times before coming to a stop in the opposite direction. His knees buckle and his body crumbles to the ground, beating the blood that is dripping out of his mouth.

My anger has now gotten a hold of me, and I am in a feeding frenzy. I reach onto a nearby 55-gallon drum of cleaning chemical and grab the nearest weapon of destruction I can lay my hands on, which happened to be a ball peen hammer. I swing it downward onto Mikey's body, landing it sharply on his torso. I wind up for a second swing, it lands on his head at the hairline, where a wide gash opens up. I can see the white flesh of the wound. And then just like that, it fills in with the red life blood of his body.

I swing two, three more times randomly and wildly landing blows on torso, shoulder and face before my guy Joe grabs me and yells "You're gonna kill him! You're gonna kill him, stop, stop!"

I lose my balance and stagger sideways and I drop the small ball peen hammer and it clinks on the concrete floor, first the metal head, then the wooden handle.

"Don't you ever grab me again, you hear me?"

"I—I thought you were going to kill him! He ain't worth it."

I regain my composure quickly. I look down and watch as the bloody pool starts to take on a more circular shape around his head. I can smell the copper aroma of his blood mix in the air with Armor All and soap. It's a weird scent, although familiar when separate.

Joe is looking a little panicked. "That's a lot of blood. What are we going to do? What if he's dead?"

I reply somberly, "Calm down, he ain't dead. Let's get him out of here." And so we did just that, only Joe didn't even realize how close *he came* to getting killed. Cause if Mikey was dead, I would have had to kill Joe too; no witnesses, period.

Just for argument's sake, I checked Mikey's nose for breath, and his neck for a pulse, and finally his pockets for my money, which he had on him—all $3,000 of it plus some more, just as I expected from a guy like him. I pulled out his keys and threw them to Joe.

"Here, go pull his jeep up to the door and open the passenger side door."

Joe was gone in a flash, and I heard the bells on the door ring as he left, and five minutes later ring, as he came back in. We dragged Mikey's 225-pound dead weight body out of the car wash and laboriously got him into his jeep, all while he was out cold. "Drive his jeep to the gym parking lot by the bakery, I'll follow you."

"Okay, but what if he wakes up?"

"Tell him you're taking him to the hospital, then take him, and make sure he keeps his mouth shut." We pull into the parking lot of the mini mall. Joe pulls into a spot in the middle of a row. As he swings the jeep into the spot it reveals the passenger side of the jeep. I can see Mikey slumped in the seat, head pulled forward and down by gravity, rolling slightly from side to side. I can see the crimson color of the blood on his face. The brake lights glow red, then go off.

Joe walks over to the driver's side of my car. "Now what?"

"Get in, let's go. Where's the keys?"

"I left them in the ignition."

"Come on, get in, I'll take you to lunch." I smile at him, but he seems glum for some reason. Who cares, I'm hungry.

By the next day the whole town knows and some of the surrounding towns too. I'm getting beeped like crazy. Everyone from the curious to the serious, which to me, is only one person, the guy who brought me in and groomed me through the years.

I call him back right away. "Hello," I reply.

"Hey, it's me."

"What's up? You got time for a cup of coffee?"

"For you, I got all the time in the world."

He laughs. He loves me like a son, but also knows there isn't anything he could ask of me that I wouldn't do. I'm as loyal as a dog to him; a vicious attack dog, but loyal.

"Okay, meet me by the club in an hour."

"Okay," he hangs up.

I follow and do the same. At the club we take a walk down the street. He asked what happened. And I hand over the monies owed from Mikey and make light of the whole attack thing but tell him everything a minute later.

"Okay, well just lay low for a few days in case he goes to the law."

"Okay, but he won't. He's too afraid, plus he knows he brought this all on himself for lying and ducking me."

"Just be careful, I don't want to lose you for nothing. I need you out here, not in jail."

"I understand."

Somebody from the gym found Mikey passed out in his car, thought he was dead, and called the cops, who called an ambulance, which took him to the hospital. It wasn't until 1998 when Mikey had gotten into some trouble with the law himself, that he told on me for his earlier injuries.

When he got arrested, I would receive ten years in federal prison coupled with other charges.

COLLECTING MY MONEY

Beep, beep, beep, beep, beep ... I pulled my beeper off my belt, pressed the button to check the number, but didn't recognize it. I picked up the house phone and dialed the number. It rang twice before a man's voice came over the line, "Roxie's, can I help you?"

I replied, "This is Little John, somebody just beeped me."

The voice replied, "Yeah, it was me."

"Me who?" I was breaking his stones. Once he said Roxie's, I knew who was calling, but I let him tell me anyway.

"It's Fredo."

"Hey Fredo, what's up?"

"We need to talk. Where can we meet?"

"Well, I'm busy, so it will have to be later or tomorrow," I replied. He belonged to the same family, but a different crew, so I was sort of being a little difficult.

"Well, that ain't good enough. I need to see you now about the guy you smacked around in the bowling alley last night!" His tone had changed and I didn't like it, but I hated talking on the phone just in case it was taped.

"Listen Fredo, I ain't discussing this on the phone," I said. "I'll meet you later or tomorrow. What's this got to do with you anyway?" I said sternly.

"That guy's a friend of mine, so leave him alone, got it?"

"Hey Fredo, no! I don't get it. He owes me eight Gs and I'm getting my money!" I slammed the phone so hard the back fell off and the battery popped out. I didn't even care.

I got dressed and left my apartment. I was going to get my money. The little punk who owed me the money had placed a bet and lost. Now because he thought he knew somebody, who thought they were somebody, he could run to him, and not pay me. Wrong! I always got my money, no matter what, and I would get it this time too. I made my first stop at my buddy's bar to get this little punk's address.

I pulled into the parking lot and felt the gravel stones crunching together under the weight of my Town Car. I didn't shut the engine off. I got out and walked to the back door, hearing the thick stones crunching under my boots. I pulled the door open and heard the low sound of the song, "Summer Wind" playing in the bar, which seemed odd to me because it was winter.

There were a few people, mostly old timers, sitting around the bar. The room was filled with smoke and smelled like stale beer. I stepped up to the wooden edge of the bar, which looked like it was there before the building was ever built. "Yo, Little John, what's up?

Jack and coke?" bartender said. His name was Billy and he was already reaching for a glass.

"No drink, Billy, I got to run. I stopped by to see if you had Mickey Cardone's address."

"Yeah, hold on. I'll write it down." He turned, stepped to the register, picked up a pen and started to write. He tore off the page and walked back, "You want me to call him for you?"

"No, it's gonna be a surprise visit," I said with a smirk. He handed me the paper, I thanked him and left, got back into my car and checked the address. I knew exactly where it was.

I could hear the doorbell ring from where I stood, outside on the porch. It was dark out by now, so the porch light flicked on. I saw Mickey walk to the door, pull it open, and turn white. I didn't say a word at first, I just punched him in the face. He staggered backwards and I stepped into the doorway. "You tried to get out of paying me by calling Fredo, you piece of ****. You got thirty seconds to get my money or I'm gonna kill you." I was pissed and the words came out sounding as much.

"I don't got it, give me a few…"

"29, 28, 27…" I pulled the gun from my waistband and pointed it at his face, "26, 25, 24…"

"Okay, okay, hold on! Don't get crazy. I'll get it! I'll get it," He said while he was holding his bloody nose. He walked away and not even five minutes later came back with an envelope with eight-thousand dollars in it. He handed it to me. I grabbed it and said, "You see how easy that was, you piece of ****. Now go call Fredo and tell him I was here." I shoved him backwards and left.

I had to go to Hoboken the following day to meet a captain and relay a message from another captain, so while I had an audience with this guy, I made it a point to bring up all that had happened over the last couple of days. Everybody who knew me, loved me, especially the old timers. I always handled business and always showed respect. I think they all actually got a kick out of me and my tactics!

Once the meeting was over, I left with the green light I had come to get. I was told to handle it how I saw fit and that Fredo had no business sticking his two cents in my business. I took it as permission to beat him into submission, so he would never stick his nose into my business again. And that's exactly what I planned on doing.

I left Hoboken, went home, called a friend and told him to pick me up. Once he got to my apartment, I laid out the ground work for our trip. We drove from my apartment over to Crooks Avenue in Paterson. We were headed over to Roxie's, Fredo's go-go bar.

We pulled right up to the front door, parked, got out and looked at each other. My breath was visible in the cold air as I said, "You ready?" My friend's answer was a simple "Yeah!" His name was Freddy too, and we had done a lot of work together over the years, so I felt comfortable having him with me.

We walked to the red door at the front of this lone building. Roxie's was situated in a farmer's market. Around it was a couple little produce stores, and behind it was a car wash that was separated from Roxie's by a set of railroad tracks. Nobody was out, it was too cold. A few cars drove by, but it was one of those cold days where everything seemed to stand still.

I opened the door and stepped in with my friend Freddy following right behind me. The place was just opening. No one was in there except three people sitting by the bar. My eyes hadn't adjusted yet, so I couldn't make them out. The bar was dark, no music was playing and it was quiet. I could smell the beer and liquor from many nights gone by. The place stunk of stale beer and Pine Sol cleaner. A young kid came over from the three that sat there, "We're not open yet, not till 3:00," he said.

"Fredo here?" I asked.

"I'll go get him," he said, as he walked to the back. Now with my eyes focused, I notice one of the two men left at the bar was a local municipal judge I knew.

"Hey Billy, how's it going? What, are you trying to warm up for court later?" I sarcastically said.

He just smiled and replied "Yeah, something like that. How you doing, John, staying out of trouble?"

"What fun would that be?" I said. As I turned away, I saw movement out of the corner of my eye. It was Fredo and he looked nervous.

"Hey, Little John, Freddy, what's up guys?"

My initial thought in my head was, *Where's the tough guy act now!* But instead, I said, "Where can we talk?"

"Over here." He walked back towards where he had come from.

I followed and told my Freddy, "I'll be right back." He just nodded in the affirmative.

Fredo pushed open a swinging door that led into a decent sized kitchen. The lights were bright and it smelled like raw hamburger meat, onions, bread and grease. He stopped a few feet ahead of me, turned and said, "What's up," as if nothing was wrong. I looked him up and down. He was short, fat and disgusting. He looked dirty. There were stains all over his shirt and his suit jacket was rumbled, as if he had slept in it. He had the whole homeless-chic thing down to a science. His hair was disheveled, and he had a seven o' clock shadow. This guy was a mess and was obviously burning the candle at both ends.

I delivered the two messages I was told to relay. He just listened nonchalantly. That is, until I said, "Fredo, before I go, you owe me an apology for the way you were talking to me the other day." I knew he would flip out and give me my opportunity to punish him. And it's exactly what he did.

"I ain't apologizing to nobody for nothing," he spewed.

I said, "Well I ain't leaving here without an apology."

That's when he blew his top and spit the words out, "I ain't apologizing to you or nobody!" He stepped forward to try and walk around me to leave, but I interpreted it as a sign of aggression. My mind was made up from before I even got here that I was going to punish him. I waited for his next step to come into range of my fists, then I heard my name from behind me.

I spun around thinking it was my Freddy or someone who was intervening on Freddo's behalf. Instead, I came face to face with a large man who was using my name and talking to me. It felt weird, cause the time seemed to stop and all I could concentrate on were his words, "John, you're not going to understand this…"

"Listen, mind your ******* business or else," I said venomously.

But he only replied in a calm voice. "John, you must listen to me. You're about to get yourself into a lot of trouble…"

I couldn't help but listen. His voice and looks were so familiar. I couldn't help thinking he meant me no harm. So, I said, "I don't understand what this has to do with you. Just leave or you will regret it."

"No, John, you're the one who will regret not listening to me. I'm you, John, and I'm here to tell you that God loves you and has a plan for you."

"Listen buddy, just leave before you get caught up in something you got nothing to do with," I said.

But he calmly continued where he left off. "God loves you, John, and wants you to do good, make correct choices and be prosperous. Listen to what He has to say in Proverbs 27:3: 'A stone is heavy and sand is weighty, but a fool's wrath is heavier than both of them.'"

I heard a noise behind me. I turned and saw Fredo storming towards me. I quickly turned back to see if the big guy who was talking about God was attacking too, but he wasn't there, he was gone. I swung back toward Fredo and without a second thought, I threw my right hand and arm at his approaching fat face. My fist slammed into his cheek. I felt my knuckles hit his cheek bone. I watched the fat on his face push back in a grotesque ripple effect. He stopped in his tracks as if he had hit an invisible wall. His knees buckled, but to his credit he stayed up, which only infuriated me further.

My wrath came in the form of several more punches. I threw crushing rights, and several devastating lefts. He fell to his knees at my feet while holding onto my jacket. In almost a crazed trance, I reached around to my back pocket to one of my favorite tools, my trusty blackjack. This beauty was an eight-inch-long by two-and-a-half-inch-wide leather encased piece of steel, with a pancake head about four inches wide, and a heavy lead nodule in the dead center. The familiar feel of its handle fit my hand perfectly. I wrapped my large hand and fingers tightly around the handle and pulled it loose from my pocket. It slid out like a samurai's sword from its sheath. I whipped it around from my back pocket to Fredo's head. Crack, the first shot rang out like a baseball player hitting a homerun. The second, third, and fourth smacks with my tool all found their marks and produced a symphonic melody that only a psychopath would have found soothing.

Fredo fell sideways to the ground half unconscious. I reached down and swatted him one last time for good measure. His response was of greater satisfaction to me than the beating. He said in a whispered voice, "I'm sorry, I'm sorry, I'm ..." and he went out like a light.

I turned and walked out of the kitchen, back into the darkness of the club and past the men sitting at the bar. My only words were to my Freddy, "Come on, let's go." I pushed the door open and stepped out into the chill of the night air. We got in Freddy's car and drove away.

MATTY

I had just spent the weekend with my beautiful little four-year-old daughter, Jackie. We played games all weekend, watched movies, went to the school playground, played hopscotch, she rode her bike, we played monster, and went to lunch at the Lodi Grill. What a great weekend. I always felt like a million bucks when I spent time with her. I was free of everything, people, drinking, drugs, women, stress, collecting money, and everything was left in the street at the curb when I was with Jackie. She was all that mattered. I even shut the phone and my beeper off while she was over. We always had so much fun laughing, going to the park behind the police station, getting ice cream, and just plain old hanging out coloring, or any of the hundreds of things we used to do.

The only problem this particular weekend was this feeling of impending doom hanging over my head. I couldn't shake this feeling that this was my weekend to die. So, with that feeling heavy on my heart Jackie and I stayed close to home Friday, all day Saturday, and Sunday.

I took Jackie home to her grandmother's house a few hours earlier than scheduled. We hugged and I showered her with kisses all over her face. She was laughing and giggling and kissing me back. "I'll see you in a couple of days, okay, my love?"

"Okay, Daddy."

"We'll do something special."

"Like what?"

"How about the zoo?"

"Yeah, can we see the monkeys, or the lions like in Lion King?"

"Yes, my love. Anything you want. I'll see you later, okay? Give me another kiss."

I bent down, kissed her again and squeezed her real tight. "Bye, baby."

"Bye, Daddy."

I walked out the side door of the house, as I did a hundred times before, only this time I felt like it would be my last. I had never felt this feeling before. It was strong. I drove back to my apartment wondering how death would come to claim me. What would be his method? All I could hope was that it was something fast, like a bullet to the back of my head. *Maybe I pissed someone off in the underworld of the mob that I ran in.* God only knows how much dirt I've done collecting money, giving beatings, fighting guys because they thought they were tough and much worse. *Maybe it will be a victim of my past or a vengeful relative or a rival gangster. I just hope it's fast.*

I made it to my apartment around 3:00 in the afternoon. I looked around the street as I passed by, did a U-turn and parked on the opposite side of the street. I got out of my Blazer truck, took another glance in both directions, crossed the street, walked up the driveway, and opened the picket fence gate which leads to an alleyway between the house and the garage. The alleyway was clear, but I was aware that something could be waiting for me at the end of the alleyway. *I doubt anybody would try anything in broad daylight.* It's best to kill at night when you can hide in the shadows and slip away in the dark.

I opened the gate, walked down the tunnel out to the other end into the sunlight and the small back yard. It was November 9th, so the air was brisk, cool and fresh to the nose. I can smell sauce and fried meatballs in the air. My land lady always made sauce on Sundays, (as do any Italians worth their weight in Parmesan cheese). I opened the door at the back of the house, and down the cement steps to another door, which led to my basement apartment.

I opened the door, walked in, and observed. It was quiet, still, and peaceful. I felt safe. I walked to my bedroom door, and straight to my California king sized bed, to lift the edge of the bed and pull out my .380 automatic pistol. I checked the slide to make sure there was a bullet in the chamber, hit the safety off and slid the gun to its familiar position on my waist.

Next, I stepped over to my dresser, pulled the top drawer open, and took out the small tin where I kept my pot. I picked up the EZ Wider papers, snapped one out of it, took a pinch of the shake in the tin, placed it into the paper between my thumb and index finger and rolled the pot into a joint. I sat on the edge of my bed, inhaled heavily, and felt the smoke burn my lungs. I held it for a minute, then exhaled the smoke along with some of the stress from this feeling of doom that had persistently hung over my head all weekend.

I sat there smoking in the peace and quiet of my sanctuary, my headquarters, my hideout, thinking of death and what form it would take to come and escort me to hell, because I knew that was exactly where I was going—straight to the fiery pit, the Devil's playground. I wondered who I'd see when I got there, a victim? Maybe some demons like in Dante's *Inferno*. I wondered if the Devil would like me and my resume of chaos and destruction.

I started to feel a little better as the weed started to take effect. My thoughts started to scatter. I touched the gun with my forearm as my arm relaxed a bit and rested on the butt of the gun in my waistband. I smoked my joint down halfway and placed it in the ashtray. I went to the fridge, pulled out the container of iced tea, and poured myself a cold glass which cleansed my pallet of the pot taste.

I went back to my room, kicked off my shoes, picked up the remote, and laid back on the huge bed. I flicked through the channels, surfing, trying to take my mind off of the thoughts of doom that were hanging in the air like the smoke from the joint in my room. I stopped on a game; I think the Giants were playing.

My mind filled with all the possibilities death had for me. I laid there in a daze seeing the football players on the screen but watching a mental picture of my funeral instead. I wondered who would come. I wondered how many of the girls I messed with would be there. *It would be funny if they all started fighting. I could see my dad and mom and my whole family just shaking their heads saying "Only John Anthony would have girls fighting at his funeral."*

"Yo Little John, Yo, John, you in there?" I hear somebody yelling at my door.

"What is it?"

"It's me, Matty."

"Come in, it's open." I hear the door open and close two seconds later. Matty is standing in the doorway to my bedroom.

"Yo, what's up. What are you doing today? Where's Jackie? Want to get some drinks, lunch, what's up?"

"Nah, bro, I'm just chilling. I just dropped Jackie off by her grandmother's and I'm just going to hang, relax, you know?"

"Come on, man, I got a pocket full of cash." He pulls it out and flashes me the wad. "We can stay local, go to Gleason's, have lunch and watch the games."

"No, really, I'm good."

"Come on, man. Come on. We'll drop my truck off by my mother's, I'll get dressed, then we'll go. What do you say?"

"I don't know bro; I feel weird today."

"Weird how, like sick?"

"No, not sick, like something is going to happen to me. I can't explain it, it's just a weird feeling."

"Okay, well some lunch and a few beers will work wonders. Let's go."

"All right, bro, I'm in. Let's go, but I ain't staying out late."

"Okay, deal."

I get up, put my shoes back on, roll myself two to three joints for the road, and we leave. I follow Matty to his mom's, and we drop the truck off. He runs in, comes right back out, jumps in my truck, and we drive to Gleason's bar. In fifteen minutes, we're there.

We park in the back, walk in through the back entrance, and are hit with the smell of steak, sour beer mixed with cigarettes, whiskey and hot wings. The lights were dim, so we closed our eyes for a second to refocus them. It's cool inside, but not cold, good drinking temperature. We find our seats after walking through the small crowd of guys and girls. Some we knew and exchanged hellos, others just got a nod or a wink.

Once seated, the female bartender comes over, "What's up guys?"

I say "Hi, sweetheart. Give me two Buds and two menus, and whatever you want," I wink. She smiles and turns to get our drinks. We look at the menus, decide on some appetizers, and two cheeseburger platters with fries. The barmaid comes back over, puts two napkins down, and places our beers in front of us. We reach for our beers. I grasped the cold glass bottle, cheers with Matty and we drink. I take a long swig of the beer, it tingles my tongue and hurts my teeth a little, but it tastes great.

Matty and I sit there for a while eating, drinking, and talking about the game, girls, and guy talk in general. Food gone, beers flowing, we decide to do a shot, then another. Now all is well, and the feeling of doom is nowhere to be found, in my new inebriated state. And with my gun in my waistband, I'm hoping somebody will try to kill me, because I'm ready! We drink some more, laugh a lot, and then we agree to leave and go to JC's across town. This sounded especially good to me because I had a thing going on with the barmaid there, Kat.

We leave, drive to JC's, go in, find our seats, and say some hellos. Kat comes over, kisses me, and we order some beers and shots. Kat is getting off soon and we make plans to go back to my apartment. The new manager is a girl I used to date. She says hi and tells the staff they're having a meeting downstairs. It's about 7:00 now. We had started drinking about 4:00.

The new shift comes on, a young kid, whom I don't really know. Kat goes downstairs to the meeting, and 20 minutes later she comes up pissed off.

"What's wrong?"

"She's trying to change my schedule and take my Sundays, this is BS."

"Don't worry, I'll handle it. You'll be fine, I promise, okay? Give me a kiss. Come on, let me walk you to your car."

"Okay, let me grab my purse, I'll be right back."

I walk Kat out to her car. We smoke a joint together and agree to meet later that night. She leaves, and I go back inside.

Now I'm sort of pissed off that my ex is trying to mess with my next. She (the ex) comes over and buys us some shots. We toast each other, me, her and Matty and she cozies up to me. "Why don't you come over tonight, I'll make you some food and we can hang?"

"I'll see, me and Matty are chilling, watching the games. When do you get off?"

"About 10:00. Think about it, okay?" She kisses my cheek and goes back to her office.

I turn back to the bar, which was empty except for me, Matty, and a few people scattered around, but I see two guys walk in that I know. We exchange looks and head nods with a what's up. All they say is a "hey" in unison. Then just like that I remembered I had wanted to kill one of them, or at the very least beat him up really bad. *No, I really want to kill him.* I remember now how he tried to get cute with Tina, Jackie's mom. She told me, and I just filed it knowing I'd see him sooner or later.

I get up and walk to the bathroom. Before I go in, I motion to the kid with the guy I want to kill, to come here. He gets up and starts to walk over. In the bathroom I tell him about the disrespect he committed against me, Tina, my daughter's mother, and although we're not together, so to speak, I'm insulted. To prove to him that I'm highly insulted I punch the hand blow dryer off of the wall and then lift my shirt and say, "You got ten seconds to get that kid and leave or I'm going to walk out there and shoot him in the face, got it?"

"Calm down LJ, calm down. We're out of here." He goes out as I watch from the crack of the door. He whispers something convincing to the guy and they abruptly leave. I come out of the bathroom feeling like a lion who just protected his territory. I proved my point for now.

Matty and I continue to party on. At one point I make the young kid who's bartending leave the bottle of liquor on the bar, and we start pouring our own drinks. We play pool and sing along to some Sinatra and Tony Bennett. We're having fun now, cracking jokes, drinking, and enjoying our little party.

At around 10:00 with our spirits high, our minds clouded, and our thoughts happy, but unclear, we decide to leave and go to my apartment. My ex continues to prod for me to come over to her house. "Are you gonna come to my house or not?"

"Okay, but what about Matty?"

"He can come and eat and take your truck home, then I'll drive you in the morning, okay?"

We walk outside, the three of us. I walk her to her car, tell her I'll follow her, and go to get in my truck. Matty is already in the driver's seat, but can't start the truck, it's flooded. "You ain't driving, I'll drive," I say. We're both drunk, but I seem better than him. He slides out of the driver's seat, and goes around to the passenger's side, and climbs in. I get in the driver's seat, the girl beeps and waves. I smile and nod, she pulls away.

I start the truck, go to put it in drive, and a voice from the back seat says, "John, you should think twice before you drive, you're drunk."

I reach for my gun and catch a glimpse of the voices face in the mirror. At first, I'm confused, but then I realize I'm not seeing double, I'm seeing an older me next to my face in the mirror. Everything is the same except his goatee is gray and mine is not, his mouth is moving, mine isn't, and Matty is asleep in his seat.

"Listen to me for a second, this is gonna be hard to understand, but I am you and I've come to give you a chance to make the right choice. Just hear me out and I'll explain. If you drive away from here tonight something bad might happen. You've been feeling impending doom hanging in the air, well this night could be what that feeling is all about."

"How did you know about that feeling, I didn't tell anybody... Who are you, what do you want?"

"I just told you, I'm coming to give you a chance at making this right choice. You are out of control and you're going to hurt someone close to you if not yourself. You know right from wrong; you don't have to drive this truck. You could call for a cab or a friend for a ride. John, God has a plan for your life. He loves you and wants to see you do good. Listen to His Word in Titus 2:11-14: 'For the grace of God that brings salvation has appeared to all men, teaching us that denying ungodliness and worldly lusts we should live soberly, right, justly and godly in the present age looking for the blessed hope and glorious appearing of our great God and Savior Jesus Christ who gave Himself for us, that He might redeem us from every lawless deed and purify for Himself his own special people zealous for good works.'"

"What the? God's word, I don't believe in God—" I say that into the rearview mirror, but spin in my seat with my gun in hand. I point it to the rear and fire a shot into the seat. I'm stunned to see the back seat is empty, nobody's there.

"What the hell is going on?" Matty jumped to attention, "Yo, what's happening?"

"Nothing, I'm just messing with you, let's go." He sits back and I put the truck in drive. My first stop is home. "Forget Tori" I tell him, "We're going to my apartment. I'll cook and you can crash on the couch, okay?"

"Yeah sure, whatever."

"Damn I forgot to call Kat."

"She'll forgive you, they all do."

"You're just jealous."

No response. Matty dozes off and I drive toward my apartment.

†

"What the!" I feel like I'm being abducted. "Get your hands off of me!"

"Hold him down strap him in!"

"I'm trying, he's too strong. Bob, grab him. Steve, hold his arm."

"Okay, I got him. He's strapped in."

"Let me go, I'll kill all of you. Get off of me." Something snaps.

"Oh crap, he broke the strap! Hit him with some Demerol, 20 ccs. Hurry up, he's going crazy!"

Red and blue lights are spinning everywhere. I can't focus my strength. I can't move. *What is this? What's going on?*

I wake up in the hospital. I hear a familiar voice. *What's my lawyer doing here? I must be dead and he's here to ID the body. What happened? Did that guy in the back seat kill me? I should have checked the back before I got in, too late now.*

"Why is he shaking like that?" my lawyer asks the nurse.

"He's trying to fight the drugs the EMTs had to give him, something to calm him down. He was too violent."

"Hey, Marty."

"Hey, Mr. Paladino. How are you doing?" my lawyer is talking to the familiar voice of my father.

"I'm all right, just trying to get some answers. What did you hear?"

"He was somewhere drinking, cause his blood alcohol level was high. They think he just passed out and crashed over by that factory at the end of River Road. His truck went under an eighteen-wheeler. I can't believe he's alive."

"Does he know the kid Matty is dead yet?"

"No, I don't think so. He's been out since they brought him in."

"John, John, you did it this time…" my father's voice is weak. I can tell he's upset, not so much with me as for me.

I'm in ICU. I wake in a daze a few days later, I can barely focus. There's a huge tube in my mouth going down my throat, and machines are beeping and buzzing all around me. One machine looks like an accordion and it's rising and falling, pushing air in and out of me. My arms are filled with needles leading to tubes that snake out of my arms and up to bags hanging on poles hovering over me at bedside. I close my eyes and fade out.

I'm lost, floating in and out of reality. I realize now I'm not dead, I'm in a hospital, but I can't move because I'm so doped up and I can't talk because of this tube down my throat. I guess I'll go back to sleep. I don't really know how long I stayed like that, but at some point during some day, at some hour, a nurse came in and she started to talk to me about the tube down my throat. I shook my head up and down. She did a few things by my bedside, then she spoke again, and I nodded. I watched as she reached for the tube. *She smelled good,* I thought to myself.

She unplugged the tube from the nozzle in my mouth. She was talking the whole time and I was just lying there trying to figure out what happened to me and where was Matty. She gently pulled the remainder of the tube out of my mouth and throat. I could feel the tube sliding up and out of me. It reminded me of pulling a rope through a pipe, only I could feel it all the way. Finally, the tube came out. I took a long breath of air and I shut my mouth for the first time in how long? I don't know. My mouth was dry. "Water."

"Go easy, just sip it, okay? You've had this tube in for a week, so go easy." The nurse pushed the straw towards my lips. I hungrily pushed my mouth out to bite at it from the bed. "Easy honey, a little at a time." The water comes up the straw slow at first. I'm so weak I can hardly suck the water up. I watch the straw fill slowly with the liquid, finally it hits the bend in the straw and pours into my mouth soaking every inch of dryness. I swallow. It goes down a little rough at first, but once my throat is well lubricated, I pull harder on the straw and try to siphon as much water as possible out of this well and into my dried-out body.

"Slow down, honey. You can have more, just go easy." The nurse pulls the cup and straw away. The straw sticks to my bottom lip for a second and breaks loose. I watch the water intently as she places the cup on the side table. My eyes are heavy.

I muster the strength to say, "Where's Matty?" Before I get an answer, I doze off.

I don't know how long I was out, but the days melted into one another. And I could hardly keep my eyes open for more than a few minutes at a time. The next time I woke up was in the medical unit in a cell in Bergen County Jail with nothing on but a paper gown. I tried to sit up, but my body wouldn't let me. I felt like a turtle upside down, struggling to right itself. My body hurt fiercely. My head was pounding, and I still didn't know what was going on.

I heard the door buzz and the lock crack as someone pushed open the solid cell door. "John, hold on, let me help you."

I sit up and look into the face of a county jail guard I know. "Garardi, what's going on?"

As he pulls me up, so I can sit on the edge of the bed, the pain sears through my body like a shot of brandy on a cold winter night, only this isn't in any way, shape, or form, pleasant. I don't think I ever felt this kind of pain encompassing my whole body.

"You had an accident. You got messed up really bad. Matty's dead, John. Do you know that? Matty's dead."

I stare at him for what seemed an eternity and finally, my thoughts started to focus, and pieces of my memory start to flood into my brain like a puzzle building itself in midair.

I start to see me and Matty at the bar, in the street driving down the road, *no wait, the guy in the back seat. He must have killed Matty and tried to kill me. What was he saying again? Something about me and him being each other. God, don't drive, a verse about soberly ungodliness, lust of the world?* I reply, "I heard Marty and my dad say something, but I've been in and out of consciousness. I thought I was dreaming, now I wish I was."

I start to get choked up. All I can think of is *I just killed my friend, what happened?* "John, can I get you anything, some food, something to drink, what?"

"Yeah, I need a phone. I can't believe this."

"Okay, hold on, let me see if the phone in the back is working. Sit tight, I'll be right back."

I sit there in disbelief thinking, trying to fit the pieces together. They're coming in slowly, but I'm still drugged up and can't focus. The scene at the accident comes filtering in. I'm sitting in my truck, I look over at Matty, he's staring at me blankly. I can't talk. All I see as I turn my head out the smashed windshield is flashing lights, reds and blues twirling, and a bunch of people all standing around looking in at me.

I hear their voices but can't make out what they're saying. The red and blue lights are accompanied by loud sirens, walkie talkies crackling, metal grinding and crunching. *What the hell. They're cutting me out of my truck!* Sparks are flying, someone looks through the smashed windshield, "Hold on we'll have you out in a minute!"

I pass out. I wake on a stretcher. I pass out again. I wake in the hospital. I pass out. I wake up here in jail, where I don't pass out again, unfortunately.

Garardi comes back in, "You okay to walk? You need help? Here, hold my arm." I reached down and he lends me his bent arm just like you would put your arm out for an old woman or an old man. I reach for it gingerly.

My body aches so badly, *but what is my pain compared to the pain Matty will never feel again because I killed him?* My eyes well up with tears. I can't believe this is all happening. My first call is to my father, but he isn't answering. My second call is to Tori, she'll know who to call for me. "Tori, it's me," I say it in such a weak voice I doubt she recognizes me, so I say, "John," just to be sure.

"Oh my God, are you okay? Where are you? What can I do for you? Oh my God, John." She starts to cry and so do I.

I manage the words "Get me out of here, please." I hang up without even waiting for her response. I feel like I'm walking through a dream. *This can't be happening. Poor Matty.*

Garardi helps me back to the cell they're keeping me in. I sit down hard, as if I just expended all my strength lifting a car off a kid. All my strength was expended, but by no feat of strength, just that walk twenty feet and those few words drained me of every ounce of strength I had in me. Garardi leaves me. "I'll check on you in fifteen. I'll bring you something to drink and eat, okay?"

"Okay, thanks." I manage those words half heartily. As I readjust myself on the bunk, I remember the searing aching pain that my body is racked with. I pull the gown across my body to reveal the damage from my chest to my hips. I'm painted black, yellow, blue, red and purple with bruises in different stages of healing, hurting and everything in between. I lightly press the bruises that coat my body in this special paint of blood just under the surface of my skin and just above my skeleton and vital organs. I lay back and just drop onto the bunk. I pass out, this time from grief and exhaustion.

"Paladino, 70 Paladino, get up. You're out of here. You're going home."

"What time is it? What's today," I ask as I struggle to sit up.

"It's about 9:30 p.m. on Tuesday, the 16th."

I see a bottle of water on the metal desk and a white Styrofoam tray. I stand, wobbly on my bare feet, reach for the water, and open it slowly as if I were turning a rusted bolt on some old machine. I put the bottle to my lips and drink. I swallow mouth full after mouth full until the bottle is 3/4 of the way empty. I put it down and say, "Where's my clothes?"

The cop, who's staring at me with compassion in his eyes, says, "Wait here. I'll grab them from booking so you can get dressed in here. You look like you're in a lot of pain."

I sit back down with so much effort I think to myself *you should have stayed up*. He's back in ten minutes, although it felt like ten hours. I get dressed with great effort. I slip on my shoes and make my way out, following the cop like a child going to the principal's office for acting up.

I stop at the desk and Officer Sullivan says, "Sign this," and hands me a pen, and slides a piece of paper in front of me. I scribble something that looks more like a doctor's signature than my own, put the pen down and look at the cop. He reached down with a mechanical movement, that no doubt he performed thousands of times, and hands me a manila envelope. "Your money, jewelry, beeper, keys and belt are in there. Want to check it?" I grab it and say "No, I'm a sure it's all there." The door buzzes and clicks.

"Go ahead, Paladino, your ride's waiting." Up until that point I never even thought of a ride. *I wonder who's here? Got to be my father, Tori?*

"John, over here... you okay? Give me that." It's my friend and running partner, Pete. He takes the manila envelope, opens the door for me and we walk out into the cold brisk November air.

I still feel like I'm in a dream, like I'm in a tunnel with no sound, no smell, just drifting along. I hear the bleep, bleep of the car alarm. He opens the door for me, I get in slowly. He shuts the door. The inside of his Caddie smells like leather and cologne. He gets in, starts the car, but doesn't say anything. I break the silence with a sob and words that are weak and frail. "I can't believe I killed Matty."

He lights a joint, passes it to me and we pull out of the parking lot on our way to my apartment. Few words are spoken, but I find out Matty's already been buried. When all was said and done, the judge gave me seven years which I have to do 85% for the accident. I went home that night and took a shower and, in that shower, I think I shed more tears than there was water coming from the pipe above. I already missed my friend. We had been together every day laughing, joking, drinking, and chasing girls. We had a lot of fun together and now because of my bad choice, my terrible decision to drive while I was drunk, Matty was dead!

I spent a month in my apartment grieving. People came and went, dropped off food, made sure I was okay. But I wasn't. I was broken because of what I did. I just didn't show it. I stayed locked in my basement apartment for thirty-odd days and I slept, smoked pot, and cried. One night, I received a call from Matty's mom.

Not knowing who it was, I answered as usual. "Hello?"

Silence answered me back. I could hear sadness in that silence, and somehow, I knew that it was Mrs. Valardi. Ice cubes in a glass gently crashed against the sides of the glass. It was an eerie silence waiting to hear this mother's voice ask me questions of which I knew I could offer no real answers. I spoke again, "Hello, hello, is anybody there?" The phone went dead. I knew in my heart she had to gain the strength to talk to the man responsible for taking the life of her youngest son, Matthew. And although we knew one another, she couldn't understand at that moment that it was an accident.

She knew in her heart that Matty was my friend. I'd been in their home, picked him up on numerous occasions, and I'd sat and eaten at their table. But at this moment I was nothing more than the object of her hate and disgust. I was the killer of her baby boy. The phone rang again. I picked it up, "Hello."

"John what happened?" That was all she asked in her cracked voice. "What happened?"

In my mind I answered *That's a good question, Mrs. Valardi.* My mouth said "I don't know, I'm sorry Mrs. Valardi."

Her voice screeched, "What happened! Tell me what happened! I need to know!"

My weak and inadequate answer was, "I don't remember the accident, all I remember is we went out for drinks and I woke up after the crash. I'm so very sorry, Mrs. Valardi. If there is anything you need, anything I can do—" silence answered me.

"I have to go. I can't talk right now." I could hear the devastation in her voice, the loss, the heartache, the blame, the sorrow. I could hear her heart breaking as we spoke and mine broke along with hers for us all.

Every day was torture for me, but what right did I have to complain? My heart, my torture was nothing compared to Matty's death and I took everything from him and everything he will ever have or be. *I was responsible for that.*

The memory of that night filtered in, in pieces too small to detect at times; the bar, drinks, gun, anger, more drinks, Kat, Tori, more drinks, Matty, me, pool table, more drinks, singing Sinatra, Bennett, more drinks, outside, cold, I'll drive, move over, start truck, guy in back seat? *Guy in back seat that looks like me said he was me, what else did he say? God loves me? Plan for me? Yeah right. Some plan, God, kill Matty, go to jail. Great plan. Thanks a lot! God, what kind of a God would let this happen, no God of mine!*

I spent the next six months living life, trying to block out the fact that I was going to jail for killing my friend. All the chaos and destruction I had committed, and this is what I was going to prison for—crazy! Kat and I moved in together a month after the accident. We set up a house, bought furniture, ate, slept, worked, planted a garden and never talked about the accident or Matty. We moved forward. I promised Kat that I'd get us a house eventually and we'd settle down. This was undoubtedly one of the most ironic times of my life. I was so happy with Kat, but so sad for the loss of my friend and the pain I caused his family.

I fought Tina in court for Jackie and won visitation. She tried to keep her from me once she knew I was with Kat. True to my word, I found a house for us. We moved in and set up a room for Jackie. I got better mentally and physically. I worked, collected here and there, and ran our social club for card games on Friday and Saturday. Life was starting to look okay. Kat and I got engaged, and we were trying to have a baby. All this happened between November 9, 1997 and April 28, 1998; six months of bliss with an undercurrent of sadness from losing my friend.

One morning, while Kat and I were in bed, getting ready to start our day, the phone rang. She answered, looked puzzled and said, "I think it's your cousin trying to be funny. He says he's the cops, look out the window." I take the phone, "Who's this?" The reply I got woke me up more than any cup of coffee could ever have.

"This is the FBI, you've got five minutes to open the door or we're coming in." I hang up, go to the window and to my surprise it looks like a scene from the movies. The street is blocked off with huge black panel vans, cop cars are there with lights on but no sound and there's cops everywhere in black with machine guns.

When they see me in the window, a cop holds up a megaphone and says, "John Paladino, come out with your hands up." I turn to Kat and quote a movie line I once heard; "You haven't lived until you heard those words." She wasn't smiling. She really didn't know all I was doing on the side or before we met. She was in shock.

I opened the door, they rushed into our living room and arrested me. They searched the house and found a gun. I was arrested for a Rico Act 21 count indictment, plus the gun. I was charged with extortion, gambling, putting a guy in the hospital, among other things.

Jackie was now about six years old. We had spent the past four years growing in love. And in our father-daughter relationship she was the world to me. But everything changed when these agents came busting through that front door. I lost everything I had put together. I lost my daughter, my beautiful girl, who by that time was my fiancé, I lost my house, cars, money, clothes, furniture. I lost my freedom for the next ten years, 120 months, 3,650 days, all for the love of money.

On April 18th, I went to court from a federal hold in Union County. Matty's family didn't come. They never forgave me, even realizing that it was an accident. We never spoke even though I wrote them all letters, Matt's mom, and two brothers. They never responded and I didn't write again. I have never stopped missing my friend.

WHISKED AWAY

The Feds flowed through the front door like water bursting a dam. I just stood there anticipating the feeling of the cold steel handcuffs being placed on my wrists. I wasn't disappointed at all as they took hold of me and placed those manacles on me and secured those irons with several clicks tightening them to ensure I was incapacitated.

I was quickly swept away as if I were the victim of a kidnapping in some third world country. I was shoved into the back of a Queen Vic car and speedily taken twenty minutes away to Newark to the federal building downtown. I was placed in a small room for questioning, but since I had nothing to say other than I would like to speak to my lawyer I was taken to a basement holding cell where I sat and watched thirteen other guys that I knew be placed one by one in the same cell with me. All this and it wasn't even 8 a.m. yet. If nothing else can be said about the Feds that's nice, I can at least say they are efficient.

We waited about an hour and a half before we all were taken into the Court. One by one our lawyers showed up and those who didn't have a lawyer were appointed one either through the public defender's office or a pool lawyer. And one by one the magistrate called us all up and one by one he placed a bail or RORed the person who stood in solemn dignity before him. Everybody was getting reasonable bails, so I felt confident I would be home for dinner. 10th, 11th, 12th guy went up, I was saved for last.

I stood in front of the magistrate behind a large dark grained wooden table, my lawyer at my side. People were milling about shuffling papers, writing unseen notes, or typing every word that was spoken on a small machine that looked more like an accountant's calculator than any typewriter I'd ever seen, but yet from all my appearances in courtrooms I knew this person to be the Court stenographer who typed everything in shorthand and to later write a full report for all to request.

My confidence level abated quickly as I listened to the Federal Prosecutor describe a monster. I couldn't believe I was the person she was talking about. She went on and on in her diatribe about what a mean and terrible person I was until finally I started to become scared of me too. I almost yelled out, *lock that psychopath up*, but quickly regained my composure, my equanimity and remained calm as the magistrate listened to the prosecutor, then my lawyer, and nonchalantly said $500,000, and hit his little wooden mallet onto the wooden block it had only seconds before rested on, as if it were a show piece.

The Court officer lead me out the same door I had walked through and back into the same cell I had vacated only thirty minutes ago. I went from the comfort of my bed, being kissed awake to the hardness of a cell, to the cushion of a courtroom chair, back to the stainless-steel bench of that cell all in approximately four hours.

There are certain little things you learn from doing time that once learned whether through hunger, lack of sleep, anger, or misery you will never forget. So although those lessons may lay dormant while you're enjoying freedom, once your liberty is taken those lessons that are better described as survival tactics automatically become buoyant once again. Certain little things like saving your bread so as not to go to bed hungry or thinking that because you're tired the lights should go out or people should be quiet. The rule of thumb in jail, is sleep when you can, not when you want to.

Anger isn't an emotion you want to wear in prison, not toward your fellow inmate or especially toward the officers. It's a sure way to get a one-way ticket to the hole, the box, the shoe. And as far as misery, it's the one emotion that would make you go hungry, lose sleep, and carry anger with you, so I learned to always try to stay the furthest from it at all costs.

So, when I found myself transported from the federal building in Newark, to Union County Jail, and into the federal hold over, I flipped the switch from street guy straight to convict in 0.6 seconds. Stripped down, put into a green uniform (which signifies I was a federal inmate—state guys wore orange) I was given a bed roll and taken to a tier and told cell three was mine. They were single cells, so I was happy about that; no bunkie talking me to death.

After about a month, I was moved upstairs to a dorm-style unit that housed about fifty guys, one of which knew a guy I knew from the streets, so he got me moved up by him where it was a little more laid back and you weren't stuck in a cell. Up there you could walk around a little since the dorm was about 200 feet long. About 3/4 of the way down there was an area for the phones separated by a five-foot-high, fifteen-foot-long wall that had the bathrooms, sinks and showers on the opposite side.

Across from our bunks were six stainless steel round tables with four attached seats and a TV bolted to the wall in this area and one at the far end of the dorm, that was the Spanish TV. I fell in quickly with a few like-minded guys and we would stay up all night playing poker, sleep all morning, eat lunch, work out, joke around, and do it all over day after day. My hopes of bail were dashed when the magistrate determined with the helpful prodding from the Prosecutor, that I was a detriment to society and shouldn't be allowed bail for fear by the government that I'd get out, kill the witness and ruin their case. So, I hunkered down.

I studied my case diligently, looked up case law and statutes, met with my lawyer when need be, and in the end, I received a sentence of 120 months and I still had state charges pending for vehicular homicide from the night I had killed Matty in the accident.

I spent a year in a dorm, never leaving unless to go to court. Other than that, the dimensions of my world were 200 X 50. Due to some legal wrangling, my lawyer got me moved to state custody, where I was sentenced to seven years, 85% for the death of Matty. The sentence was to run concurrent (together) to the Feds 120 months, so while my state time ran, so did the first seven years of my federal sentence.

Prison to prison and its draconian practices hardly changed from decade to decade. Guards turn keys, gates get opened, gates get closed, guards turn keys, nothing to it but to do it, that's time of course. You can do the time or you can let the time do you. I chose to do the time by keeping myself busy. I would work out, read, write, answer letters, use the phone, any and everything I could do.

I spent my second year locked up in a state prison called Southwoods, and true to its name, it was south and in the woods. I did okay at first. I joined a culinary class thinking I'd be cooking and eating my class work, but to my dismay, all we did was book work. And I don't care how you season a culinary cookbook, it's never going to taste good, so I quit.

I concentrated on working out and eating. I soon became huge and strong along with the moniker of prison chefs. You have to learn how to make the food in prison taste good or else you could become anorexic. Needless to say, I learned a long time ago in prison that you don't eat so much for taste, as you do to just not be hungry, hence my 300-plus frame.

Due to poor judgement and a bad attitude, I only lasted at Southwood State Prison (SWSP) for a year before I got into a fight with one, then several officers and found myself in NSP, Northern State Prison, which resides in Newark, New Jersey, thankfully close to home. I was given thirteen months for an .002 infraction and it was the best time of my bid (sentence) thus far. Single cell, had my TV, my radio and even got my hands on a word processor. So, my thirteen-month stay in ad-seg (administrative segregation) was fine by me.

I left NSP on September 18, 2001, three days after my 33rd birthday. I was headed for one of New Jersey's most infamous prisons (due to my own request), Rahway State Prison, or as it's now known EJSP (East Jersey State Prison) but better known to the men who were held there as "The Belly of the Beast." I got to Rahway at about 10 a.m. As the van pulled into the parking lot, I looked up at the huge dome that was the cap of this prison. A huge half of a ball that reminded me of the ancient Greek Pantheon, only instead of housing gods the Pantheon housed killers, rapists, thieves, arsonists, and demons and I'm not just talking about the inmates.

The dome was originally a golden color due to it being made of copper sheeting, but over the decades of weather abuse it was now a tainted ugly dull green, the kind of green you saw in vomit. The van pulled through the security gates and parked at a side door. The door was flat gray, housed by red bricks. I was taken out of the van over to the door. A button was pushed that obviously rang somewhere in the depths of the Beast's belly.

The metal door clicked and the cop on my right pulled it open. We entered a small hallway. I noticed the floors were immaculate. They reflected as if they were water. We turned right, climbed five steps and came to an antiquated gate where an officer sat behind a glass window.

It looked like we had just pulled up at a drive-thru window of a bank. The officer on my left side gave a folder with my commitment papers inside into a stainless-steel drawer, the drawer was retracted and I was maneuvered over in front of the window. I was about to ask for my fortune to be told when a voice said, "State number?"

I replied, "311068."

Voice again, "DOB?"

"9-15-65."

Voice again, "Social?"

I recited my social, to which the Voice replied, "Welcome to the Belly of the Beast."

The gate was opened by an officer that had been standing out of view. He stuck his oversized key into the lock, turned it and pulled the barred gate open. I was escorted through the gate into a large rotunda where two large cages stood, each capable of holding ten to fifteen men.

I was walked over to a room on the left where the two officers took off the handcuffs, cuff belt and shackles. Only for me, due to my size, I had leg shackles on my wrists and plastic zip ties around my ankles with shackles attached to them. Once I was unhooked, I was strip searched again for the second time that morning, once leaving NSP and now entering EJSP. I've been in relationships where the women haven't even seen me naked as many times as I've been strip searched over the years!

Now on this side of the gate the same officer at the window who questioned and answered me was at the same kind of window, only this side of the gate. "Paladino," he called me through the slot where paperwork was handed back and forth. I stepped over to the window expecting my fortune this time, but instead, he slid a small piece of paper out and on it was written "two down four cell-bottom."

The two officers who transported me picked up their hardware (shackles and cuffs) and left out the gate we had come in through. I was left standing there with this small piece of paper in my very large hand. "Paladino, go to the far gate and wait, an officer will let you in," were the words that filtered out from the fortune teller's window.

I did as I was told, and waited about five minutes before a guard on the other side came, opened the gate and asked me, "Where you housed at?"

I replied, "Two down cell four."

He pointed to his left, which was my right. "Over there, report to the officer at the desk."

I didn't say anything, I just walked into the opening like it was the mouth of the Beast whose belly I'd be in.

My five years at Rahway went well. I stayed out of trouble for the most part. I lifted and became one of the top three strongest men in the prison. I played football, a flag league with hitting, and tried my best to send somebody to the infirmary every chance I got. Most weekends I was successful.

From Crime to Christ

Then on April 5, 2005, my seven-year sentence was fulfilled and I was released, but not free. Since I still had time left with the Feds, I found myself sitting in one of those cages I had first seen upon my arrival to the Belly of the Beast waiting for the US Marshals to come and pick me up and take me to the Feds. I wasn't disappointed.

The Marshals showed up at 9 a.m. stripped me, cuffed and shackled me and took possession of me from the State of New Jersey. I was driven to a federal hold over in Brooklyn, where I was stripped upon arrival and housed for two weeks. I wound up on a unit with a boss of a crime family. We sat and talked daily until the morning I left.

I was taken to Philly for two days, same routine, stripped leaving, stripped coming, then after two days I was loaded onto a converted Greyhound Bus, cuffed, and shackled in a heavy gauge paper uniform, taken to an airfield where several other inmates were taken off a plane, and placed onto the bus. We then drove to West Virginia where we were deposited at a federal penitentiary called Hazleton.

This prison was surrounded by seven layers of razor wire, stacked as high as it was deep, then a twelve-foot-high chain link fence, more razor wire, another twelve-foot-high fence, and a watch tower at every corner of the building that also acted as a wall. All this before we even get into the place. I thought to myself, *ain't nobody getting out of here*. We were checked in, stripped down, fed, and housed.

The federal system was a whole other animal compared to state prison. First off, it is filled with guys from across the country. Second, it is plagued by gangs. Third, it is very segregated, especially in the mess hall, white tables, black tables, Mexican tables, Chinese tables, etc. Even the housing was segregated, whites with whites, and so on. I got a job in the Rec Department, worked out daily, ran the wellness room, went to school, and got my GED. I graduated valedictorian, gave a speech, and tried my best to mind my business. It didn't always work, and people got hurt, but for the most part I just did my time.

I was released on February 13, 2007 and told to report to a halfway house in Newark where I had to stay for four months.

RELEASE FROM FEDERAL PRISON

Two weeks before my scheduled release from the federal penitentiary in West Virginia, I sat in my cell reading, writing, and making beaded necklaces. We were on lock down because an inmate stabbed a guard in the neck with a shank, so here I sat trying to keep myself busy.

It's funny how much you can do in an eight by twelve cell through the course of the day. I'd get up early, work out, eat the breakfast that was sent through the slot in my cell door, take a bird bath in the sink, (while on lock down it would sometimes be a week before you could get a shower), write some letters, read, eat lunch when it came through the slot, write some more, listen to my Walkman, work out again, take another bird bath, eat dinner when it came through the slot, then make necklaces until lights out, go to bed, and get up to start it all over again. A perpetual ground hog's day!

I actually thrived in solitude because mentally I found myself to be stronger than most. I saw guys cry and beg not to go to the hole or be locked in because they couldn't stand to be alone with themselves. I loved it though. At one point I did thirteen months straight in the hole. I'd also done little stints, ten days, thirty, ninety days, and every time I actually liked it. The one thing I hated was that when you went to the hole you lost your cell and all your property got tossed into garbage bags. But when you're locked down, you stay in your cell with all your property, so living is a little more comfortable, but you've still got to be strong mentally.

I almost counted it as a blessing that I left during the lock down for two reasons. First, when you get short, (that means you're going home soon), people start acting differently around you; trying to be tough, smart, rude, and at times, disrespectful. I don't know why that was, I could only guess they were envious or jealous. The second reason was that I wanted to kill a guy who had stolen from me right before the lockdown. I couldn't prove that he did it, but every instinct told me I was right. The rule of thumb in the pen, was to stab first, and find out facts later. At least you'd send a message, "don't steal from me."

It took me those two weeks to really get it through my head, that after nine and a half years from April 28, 1998, until February 13 of 2007, I was finally getting out. I couldn't wait.

On February 13, at seven in the morning, two guards showed up at my cell, "Paladino you ready?"

I said one word, "Yeah!"

"Stick your hands out the port backwards."

I turned and bent down so I could fit my hands out of the port. I was so big only one hand fit out. They had to reach in and put the other ankle cuff on my wrist. (Handcuffs don't fit me, so the cops have to use ankle shackles as cuffs for me.)

As soon as I stepped out, the 128 men erupted, yelling my name out in whistles and cheers. "Little John, yo man, be good out there!" "Stay strong, soldier!" I got along with almost everybody, so the well-wishes were many.

The huge unit was empty except for me and the two guards and the faces staring out at me from behind the cell doors. I was led to the hallway that ran behind the housing units and then down a long, huge walkway, which brought us down to Control. There, along with my escort, I was buzzed through a double locking door, into a foyer until the door behind us was closed and locked. Then, and only then, did the door to the lobby buzz open.

We walked out into a lobby that looked like it could be a hotel somewhere in New York City. Marble decked the floor, leather chairs and benches sat empty. Flower pots decorated the area with plants and flowers. The walls had paintings, there was an American flag in the corner, and even the air seemed free out there, compared to what I was breathing while behind the wall. The tension was so thick only fifty yards on the other side of where I stood now, that I really started believing it could be cut with a knife. This air smelled so different—fresher, cleaner, filled with more oxygen somehow.

"Turn around."

The cuffs came off and I brought my arms around in front of myself and rubbed my wrists thinking to myself that I'd never let a pair of them be put on me again! *I'd rather be dead.*

I sat in the lobby staring out the front doors, watching the snow fall heavily to the ground. The night before, there was a huge snowstorm. The flakes I watched were the size of cotton balls floating down and piling up. I heard footsteps come up behind me, then the voice, "Mr. Paladino I see you're leaving us today. I hope your stay here at Hazelton Penitentiary was a pleasant one, and I hope we never see you again. Do the right thing out there," the Warden said with one breath.

"I will," I said, as I turned to see him walk past me toward his office. I turned back to the snow. There was a lone guard now at a front desk, "You getting picked up, Paladino?"

"Yeah, they should be here any time now." I had made my plans weeks ago. Two of my friends were coming down to get me. They were going to stay overnight in a hotel and pick me up in the morning. I knew they would be there, come hell, or high water, or a snowstorm. Just as the guard was saying, "If they don't show, you're going to have to go back to your cell ..." a black SUV pulled up right in front of the double glass doors.

I held my breath for a second as the front driver side door opened, and out stepped my friend Kelsey. I saw my other friend, George, get out and walk around the truck. He was smiling widely as they walked toward the glass door from the outside. Seeing them, I walked out that door and took in the biggest breath I had breathed in almost ten years.

My lungs burned as I took in as much of that cold, clean, free air. I looked up as giant flakes of snow hit my bald head and face. I felt like I had just been pushed out of the womb. We all shook hands, exchanged some hugs and climbed into their truck.

I sat in the front passenger seat. The truck was warm and had that new car smell. I cracked my window so I could still smell the fresh air. The cold brisk air was intoxicating. I couldn't get enough.

The SUV slowly rolled away down the long winding driveway, past a huge parking lot with two entrances, one marked "visitors," the other marked "employees." The long driveway snaked its way down to a road. We sat in silence for a while at the stop sign until I said, "Get me out of here."

Release from Federal Prison

My friend Kelsey pulled out on to the roadway. We carefully drove down that mountain in West Virginia. The roads were wet and covered in slush and snow. A huge plow drove past on the opposite side of the road splashing dirty slush and snow onto our windshield. The wipers had to work overtime to clear the wet mess from the windshield. Then, a second plow came by, and repeated the same dousing as the first.

My friend George, sitting in the back seat, was telling me from the back, how an old girlfriend, Tori, had sent me some clothes, a digital camera, and a cell phone in a black duffel bag in the back. I told George to give me the phone. He handed me a white Virgin Mobile cell phone wrapped in a hard-plastic covering. I also received a nice little card and instructions from Tori to call her right away, and that she was sorry for not picking me up herself, but she was in Aruba on vacation, awaiting my call.

I opened the phone, and put it into the charger, at Kelsey and George's instruction. I asked for George's phone and marveled at how small cell phones had gotten over the years I was away. When I left in '98, they were big, gray, boxy, and very expensive. Everybody still had beepers back then, only a few people had cell phones. So, holding this small phone was so surreal—I felt like Captain Kirk calling Scotty to beam us up. I barely knew how to use it.

Kelsey asked if I was hungry and said we could stop for something to eat. "Yeah, I could eat something, definitely," I replied. We sat in silence most of the way down that mountain, which I had learned while in Hazelton Penitentiary, was the second highest peak in West Virginia, a half mile high. We made it down to a small town, found a little restaurant, and went in and had a great lunch, even though I felt like everybody was looking at me knowing I'd just been released from prison after nine and a half years.

We enjoyed a country-style lunch, fried chicken, pulled pork sandwiches, and lots of fries. I had almost forgotten food could taste so great. The abundance of flavors overcame my barren taste buds, and I savored every bite. We got back onto the highway full and satisfied. The snow continued to fall, and the roads continued to be cleared. We took our time driving.

Although I had been released from the Pen, I stillhad an obligation to fulfill with the Federal Government. I was released four months early to a halfway house in Newark, New Jersey, which is where I was expected to be within six hours. The staff would estimate your travel time based on where you were coming from, but with the weather being what it was,I decided to call the number on my release paper and let them know I might be late. They were very understanding and said, "No problem, take your time, and be safe."

So, with that pressure off our back, we did just that, we took our time. I made calls to my father, mother, and sister. They were all elated that I was out. I called a few friends, and finally got in touch with Tori in Aruba. She wanted me to fly out the next day, but I explained I couldn't because of my halfway house obligation. We left off that we'd talk again later.

I sat staring out the window thinking how I couldn't believe I was out, and basically a free man. I couldn't believe I had made it out of some very bad prisons with minimal trouble, and not been hurt, or lost my mind. I watched as the trees went by in a blur. I stared into other cars wondering where they might be going and I talked with my friends who were updating me what I had missed out on. I came to find out that not much had changed, even in nine-and-a-half years. Everybody was still drinking at the same bars, some people had gotten married, or divorced. Some died. But the majority were still basically maintaining the same routines.

Release from Federal Prison

We drove and drove. We stopped to fuel up a few times. Kelsey and George switched driving duties. I even closed my eyes for a little while to catch a cat nap. Finally, when we got about an hour from Newark, I gave an old friend a call. "Chel, it's me. You home?" I said.

He replied "Yeah, I'm here. You coming to get me?" I could hear the smile in his voice. We did a few years together in Rahway, and used to play cards out in the big yard.

Chelton was about 85 years old when I last saw him, and still big. He was about 6'3, and 300 pounds, but he looked like about 20 years younger than his actual age. I told him we were about an hour from Newark and that I would call him when we got into town. When we got onto Broad Street I called and we went to pick up Chelton, up on Irving Turner Boulevard. We pulled into the parking lot of his apartment building and I saw him right away, standing there smiling.

We shook hands and gave each other a hug. "You look good," I told him, and he gave me a similar compliment. We got in the truck and decided to go to Murray Street to Iberia Princess Restaurant. We walked in and were hit with the smells of Brazilian Rodizio (barbeque). A huge fire pit was blazing at the front of the place, skewers of meat, sausage, shrimp, chicken, and steak were all roasting on the open fire. The aromas were heavenly.

The place was decorated for Valentine's Day. I suddenly remembered, to my dismay, that I was coming home to no one, but then I immediately remembered that's just how I wanted it.

We all had the Rodizio. The waiter brought skewer after skewer of chicken, sausage, steak, shrimp, even scallops, until we told him to stop. We must have eaten a sow, a few chickens, a pig, and a net full of shrimp and scallops. We also ordered a cheesecake, flan, ice cream, and tiramisu for dessert. I enjoyed every bite of every single thing I ate. Then it was time to report to the halfway house.

It was about 8:30 p.m., and it was cold and dark. We drove down a long stretch of road until we saw the street sign for Toler Place. Kelsey drove us to the end of the very short street, which was a dead end. The first hundred feet of the street was flanked by two buildings, one on each side. On the left there was a decent sized parking lot, and on the right, a trailer-like building, set back off the road and surrounded by a high razor wire fence with a turnstile gate entrance in the middle. Kelsey pulled up right in front.

We all climbed out and walked to the back of the SUV. "Well, this is it. Thanks for coming to get me. I appreciate it," I said. We all exchanged handshakes and hugs. I felt like I was going on a cruise or back to jail. Kelsey opened the back of the truck so I could retrieve the duffel bag Tori had sent me. I unzipped it and rummaged through the large black bag. Inside there were cosmetics, soap, toothpaste, deodorant, a toothbrush, razors, shaving cream, socks, boxers, T-shirts, a set of sweatpants, a sweatshirt, a digital camera, and a cellphone. I zipped up the bag, flung it over my shoulder, said a few more goodbyes, and walked through the revolving gate.

I think that had to be the hardest part of reporting there; stepping through the gate from the free side to the restricted side. It was as if I were a bird who had escaped his cage during the day, but willingly went back to it at the end of the night. Every instinct in my body told me not to walk through that gate. Thankfully, my head, and not my heart, ruled the moment.

Once on the other side, I found myself faced with a door at the top of six wooden steps. I walked forward wondering what this last leg of my journey would be like. At the top of the steps there was a door, and next to the door, a small window like at a drive through for a bank. All I could think of were the old amusement park fortune teller machines. I wondered if I was going to be told some prophetic revelation on the back of a ticket, but to my dismay, no one was sitting there. A small sign on the wall stated, "Ring bell." It was placed over a small black button.

I stepped to the side and pressed the button not once, but twice. I was surely tempting fate. Not two seconds went by and a rotund black woman popped out from behind the door that led into her booth. "Can I help you?" she said, as if I were interrupting her.

"Yes, I was told to report here to the halfway house," I said in an even voice.

"Which one, Honey, we got two here. Federal or state?" she replied.

"Federal," I said, as I held up the papers I was given when I left the Penitentiary.

"Side door on the right," she said as she turned and disappeared back through the door. I stood there for a second, turned, headed back down the stairs, and stopped as Kelsey, George and Chelton were all staring at me from inside the SUV. "What's the matter, they don't want you?" They all smiled and laughed.

"They said I could leave," I said. And for a second all their faces contorted into confused looks.

"Really?" Kelsey asked.

I replied, "No, not really. I got to go to the side door. I'll see yous (sic) later." I turned and walked to the side door. This time, there were four steps and a double door to my right. I climbed the steps and stared through the slotted windows. The inside of the large room was bright right inside the doors. Only feet away was a metal detector. To the right, some tables and a desk lined the wall. Further up on the right were a filing cabinet and a small cubicle where an older light-skinned lady sat.

The room was empty other than the woman in the small cubicle. I pulled on the door, but it was locked. The woman looked up, held up a finger for me to wait, leaned over, and hit a button. The door clicked and I pulled it wide and stepped into the heated room from the cold night air. I stood there for a second waiting for some command or instructions. That's what prison will do to you. After years, you learn to follow orders, instructions and commands. You learn to wait.

Finally, she walked over, "You must be Mr. Paladino. We've been expecting you," she said in a soft voice.

"Yes, ma'am, that would be me," I said with a smile, which in turn brought a smile to her face. I dug in my pocket and pulled out my release papers. She took it and told me to have a seat in the chair by the desk as she walked around it and sat in a black swivel chair behind a computer monitor. I sat silently as she punched keys on the keyboard.

"Okay, let's see ... You were released this morning from Hazelton Penitentiary. You served 120 months. Your date of birth is 9-15-65. Your social security number is ... Your address of record is 196 Denton Avenue Clifton, New Jersey. Phone number is ... and your stay with us is for four months, which means you will be here until, let me see, ... June 8th." She said all of that more to herself, than to me. I just sat there staring out the window behind her and watched as the snow continued to fall.

I was processed in and given a bed number in a dorm at the back of the building. Before she showed me to my bed area, I was given a breathalyzer, fingerprinted, and photographed. By this time a few people had come through the door from outside, and two employees came from beyond the double doors. They were checking people in and looking through their bags while they signed into a book.

"Okay, let's get you settled in. Oh, by the way, I'm Mrs. Jackson. I mostly work second shift. If you have any questions, feel free to ask them. Otherwise, I'll explain the rules." She went onto explain the inner workings of the place. If you wanted to go anywhere, you had to fill out a request form stating where you wanted to go, why you wanted to go, what time you wanted to go, what time you were coming back, and how you were going to get there and back. It had to be dated and signed and submitted at least four days prior to the date you wanted to go.

Other than work, you basically were expected to sit in the halfway house for the first month. Then, as long as you paid 25% of your gross income, you were allowed a series of furloughs; the first furlough was two six-hour passes. The second, two twelve-hour passes, and the third, was a weekend pass from Friday 9 p.m. until Sunday 9 p.m. After completing that phase of halfway house protocol, you were evaluated for the next phase, which was home confinement. You would be fixed with an ankle bracelet and given a curfew which had to be adhered to stringently. I remembered guys who had done this, complain that staff members would call in the middle of the night to see if they were home, and then would tell them to stick their head out the door so they could verify, because they were sitting outside the house in their car.

Mrs. Jackson showed me to my dorm room. We walked through the double doors into a long hallway with doors on either side of the hall. We made our way down the glossy covered tiles, which shown so brilliantly from buffing that they looked as if they were actually wet. I looked into every door we passed; most were small offices. One was a large conference room with a huge table in its center circled by comfortable looking chairs. I recalled how over the nine-and-a-half years, I had sat on only steel chairs or concrete benches, and that the only thing that provided any semblance of comfort, was the thin mattress on my bunk—a four-inch foam plastic covered mat. No wonder my back hurt.

"Okay, this is it," Mrs. Jackson said as we stopped at another set of double doors. "You have to hit the buzzer to gain access in and out of all the main doors," she stated, as she hit the buzzer. The door clicked and we walked into another section with guys coming and going in different directions.

"Hey Mrs. Jackson," several guys said.

"Mrs. Jackson my pass was denied," another said.

"Okay, hold on a minute 'till I get this gentleman settled in, then I'll see what's going on."

The area I stood in was a common area with a table, a bookshelf, and a nook for a washer and dryer. Mrs. Jackson walked forward, and she pointed out another area on the right as the bathroom. Then she turned right again down another short hallway with a door at the end. As she opened it, she said in a loud voice, "lady in the room!" This room was the biggest I had seen yet. It housed at least a hundred men. Bunk beds lined both walls. She stopped and said, "Pick a bed, we're not full yet, so you can have your choice." I chose the bed at the far end of the room against the wall, and naturally, a bottom bunk.

"Okay, Mr. Paladino, you're all set. If you need anything, I'll be up front." She turned and walked out. I went to my bed and sat down on it. I looked around and saw several guys sleeping. A few were sitting in their areas reading or listening to music on their iPods. I unpacked and realized I needed bedding, sheets, a blanket, and a pillow. I walked out back through the labyrinth of hallways up to the

Release from Federal Prison

common area and saw a staff member, whom I asked for a bed roll. He told me to sit tight and he would check.

I met a few guys who were standing around. A couple of them filled me in on the rules, and the staff, and the inner workings of the place. I listened, got my bed roll, made my bed, and went to sleep.

The next day was Valentine's Day. I didn't have a sweetheart to call or celebrate with, so I wasn't worried about calls or visits. I was getting the lay of the land.

I found out that up by the front entrance there was a small computer/library room, some offices for staff, and a TV room. I got up early, got dressed, made my bunk, and washed up. I went out to the front common area that had a few vending machines I hadn't noticed the day before. I bought a honey bun, and an iced tea, and went to the TV. I sat there and watched the blank screen as I ate my breakfast.

I had no choice but to sit there in silence, because I couldn't figure out how to turn on the TV. I could only laugh to myself. I later found out that the place was deserted because everybody went home on the weekends on furloughs. I also found it funny that they had counts in the halfway house, so when I was asked to go to my area, I went. It had been engrained into my physical and mental state, that at certain times of the day, I had to be counted. It had now become so much a part of my day, that I often thought that when I eventually got home, that I'd robotically go stand by my bed at a certain time every day to be counted.

At around 2:00pm on Valentine's Day, I started to feel sick. I had blurred vision and a terrible pounding headache. I knew right away that it was probably my blood pressure because of the Brazilian food the night before. The one thing about prison that was good, was that they provided regular medical exams, checkups, vaccinations, and lots of pills and creams to combat illnesses and pain. Since I have high blood pressure, I was monitored monthly for any signs that my medication wasn't working, or that I wasn't doing my due diligence with proper eating and regular exercise.

But when I was released the day before, I wasn't given pills to take along with me. So that meal, which was undoubtedly filled with all kinds of seasonings and tons of salt, along with the lack of pills that morning, led to me feeling like crap. My head felt like two large jackhammers were being used over my eyes. I couldn't take it, so I went to the front desk and told the man who was there, that I need to go to the hospital. At first, his eyes registered with suspicion. He undoubtedly thought I wanted to get out to go and meet a girlfriend, but my persistence and doggedness won out over his suspicious mind. They had no medical services at the halfway house.

After conversing with his fellow staff members, they decided I could take a cab, at my expense, to Beth Israel Hospital in Newark, and go to the emergency room. Then, once at the hospital, I had to call every hour to let them know I was still there. I agreed. I quickly found out how to manipulate the furlough system due to this health issue. After that, my passes were solely to get out and have sex.

They called the cab, and I was driven to the emergency room in Newark. I walked to the large glass door, stepped on the giant black mat, and watched the door slide open with a hissing sound. It reminded me of a door on a space craft in a movie. I went in and walked to the front check-in counter where a young black girl sat chatting it up with a tall security guard. When she finally noticed me, she said, "Can I help you?"

"Yes, I don't feel well. My blood pressure is through the roof. Can I see someone?"

"You got insurance?"

"No."

"Well, fill this out." She handed me a clipboard with a form on it and a pencil attached by a piece of string and tape. I took it, sat down, and filled the form out. Once I was done, I gave it back to her and she told me to have a seat. I sat and watched her get up, go to a side door, step through it, then five seconds later come back and sit back behind her counter and continue with the security guard right where she had left off, without missing a beat.

I was the only white person in the room. I felt like all eyes were on me, not because I was white, but because I had stepped out of a federal penitentiary just 24 hours ago. I finally heard my name being called, "Paladino, John Paladino, to window four." I looked up as the woman's voice filtered into the air and drowned out the noise in the room including the TV that was hanging from the wall in the corner.

I looked over to my left and spotted the four windows with chairs placed in front of them, and instantly I had a flashback to my time in the hole at Northern State Prison back in '98. I walked over and sat in the chair that was in front of window four. A middle-aged, nicely dressed black woman was sitting behind the glass like a teller in a bank.

She smiled and greeted me and then proceeded to ask me about ten questions or so, while punching keys on a keyboard that was sitting on a pulled-out drawer. She stared at the screen and never missed a key as she hit them. I sat listening to the rhythm of the keys and saying yes to her questions and answering in more depth when I needed to. It took all of ten minutes before she looked up, smiled, and said, "You can go back to your seat and wait for a nurse to call you. Good luck."

I went back to my seat and sat there watching everyone busy texting or making calls on their little cellphones. It was crazy seeing how prevalent they had become, especially since when I went to prison back in '98, everybody had beepers. Cellphones were too expensive and too bulky. But now in 2007, everyone had small little phones that could easily fit in their pocket, like a pack of gum.

My name was called again, "Paladino, John." I stood and walked towards a nurse holding a clipboard, and thought to myself, *either I've been away too long, or the women in this hospital are all attractive.* "Come with me, please," she said in a sweet voice. I followed her into a room off the side of the waiting room. "I just need to get some vitals from you, okay?"

"No problem," I said.

She directed me to a chair, and I sat down while she busied herself putting on gloves, and a stethoscope around her neck. She sat in front of me, pulled a blood pressure cuff from beside herself, and put it on my arm. As she leaned in, I could smell her perfume. It had a floral sweet aroma to it. I watched her perform the task effortlessly. It was obvious she had done this a thousand times before.

She looked up into my eyes, "Your pressure's high, 170/100." She wrote it down and proceeded to take my pulse and my temperature and then told me to follow her. I followed her out of the room, and back into the waiting room where she opened a door to the right, and we walked into the epicenter of the hospital; the real ER where all the action took place. The waiting area was where they kept the less severe injuries, and of course, the people without any insurance, so I wondered how I got treated so quickly. Only about thirty minutes had passed from the time I got out of the cab until then. "Sit right here and the doctor will see you in a minute," she said, and then melted away into the hustle and bustle.

Release from Federal Prison

In a chair next to mine, sat an older man with his hand wrapped in gauze on a gurney. A few feet away, laid an old woman who was softly moaning to herself. A young Spanish nurse walked over and patted her arm, "You okay, Millie? The doctor will be here soon, Hon." She looked over at me and smiled. I smiled back. "Excuse me, Miss," I said.

"Yes?" she replied.

"I have to make an important call. Can I use your phone?" I asked.

"Over there on the wall, is a house phone. Pick it up and dial 5, then your number," she instructed.

I got up, dug in my pocket, and pulled out the card they gave me at the halfway house. Ring, ring, ring, ring, ring. "Toler House, Mrs. Greenly speaking."

"Hi, this is Paladino calling in from the hospital."

"Okay, Paladino, how long will you be?" she asked.

"I'm not sure, I haven't been seen yet."

"Okay, call back in an hour," she said. She hung up and so did I. I went back to my seat and watched the flurry of activity.

A thin, medium height white woman walked up to me with a clipboard in her hand. She looked up from the clipboard and over her snakeskin patterned glasses and said "Hi, I'm Dr. Tyndale. It says here your blood pressure is very high. Do you normally have high blood pressure?"

"Yes."

169

"Okay, I'm going to give you a 50 milligram Diovan and have you sit in this room over here." She pointed and walked toward a small room. I stood up and followed her. I towered over her, but still walked behind her like a little puppy. My head was still pounding furiously. "Sit in here, I'll be right back" she said, as she turned and walked away.

I stepped into the small room and couldn't help but take measurements of the square footage. After living in a cell for almost ten years, you notice things like the size of rooms more often than you would like to admit. This room was definitely the size of my cell, eight by twelve. There were two cushioned armchairs, a small end table with magazines on it, and a small refrigerator in the corner. TV played softly from its perch in the corner.

I was starting to get hungry and although I still had a smashing headache, my stomach was growling for food. My body was still on schedule with prison time, where we ate between 3 p.m. and 4 p.m. every day like clockwork.

Dr. Tyndale stepped into the doorway holding a small paper cup of water and an even smaller paper cup with a pill in it. "Here you go, Mr. Paladino. Take this and sit here for a while and we'll see if we can't get your blood pressure under control." She stepped forward and held out both cups.

The doctor was just about to turn when I spoke, "Excuse me, Dr. Tyndale, but how long do I have to sit here?"

"About thirty to forty minutes and I will have a nurse take your vitals again to see if they're normal. Why? Are you in a hurry?" she said, with a half-smile.

"Well, actually Doctor, between you and I, I'm in a halfway house and they stop serving dinner after 4 p.m. and I can't miss that," I said sheepishly.

"Sit tight, Mr. Paladino, and I'll make sure you get something to eat." She smiled and walked out.

I sat there for about thirty minutes watching TV, but more so, all the people who passed by the door. Finally, a cart came through the door followed by a bubbly nurse who cheerfully asked me how I was feeling. "Fine, the headache is finally going away," I said.

"I'm going to take your blood pressure to see if it's gone down." After a few moments, she smiled with satisfaction and said, "It's way better than before, now it's 128/89. You have to be careful with your B-P, it's the silent killer."

"Thank you, I will," I said. She pushed her cart out, and two minutes later, Dr. Tyndale stepped back into the room with a bag. "I got you something to sit here and enjoy, then I'll let you leave."

"Oh, thank you so much, I appreciate you very much."

She said, "You're welcome," and left. I opened the bag to find a huge plate of fried chicken, mashed potatoes, and a vegetable. She even brought an iced tea for me to wash it all down. I was in my glory. It took me no time at all to devour the meal. I cleaned up and poked my head out of the room.

The doctor just happened to be coming in, "How do you feel?"

"Great," I said, "thanks to you."

"Okay, well your blood pressure is down. Here is a script for some medicine. There's a pharmacy down the hall by the gift shop where you can fill it. And go see your family doctor if you have one, or make it a point to get one, okay?"

I said, "Okay Doc, I will. Is that it, can I go now?" I asked.

"Yep, you're free to go."

"Thanks again, Doc, and happy Valentine's Day."

I found my way to the pharmacy, handed the prescription over the counter, and was told I'd have to wait twenty minutes. I walked over to the gift shop and bought a $30.00 box of chocolate in a heart-shaped box, along with some gum, and a paper. I went back, picked up the pills, and found my way back to the ER desk where all the nurses stood along with Dr. Tyndale. I put the candy down and thanked them all one last time for being so nice to me. "Happy Valentine's Day, Ladies," I said, as I walked out back to the waiting room.

I found a pay phone, called the halfway house, and reported in, and told them that I was coming back. I called a cab and waited by the door. It pulled up, I got in, and went back to the halfway house. This was my second day out of prison and the taste of freedom was inviting. I wanted more freedom, more people, more girls.

Back at the halfway house, I quickly learned the ropes, and became familiar with the staff and other residents. My dad came by with some clothes for me, a couple of sweat suits, some towels, and bed linens. I stowed the items in my locker and floated around from the TV room to my bed area. I had a job lined up back in the union as a carpenter, but when I found out that 25% of my gross pay would be taken weekly, (which is half of my net), I contacted a buddy who got me a job with him at a furniture warehouse making $9.00 an hour instead. I figured I only had four months to do in the halfway house, so I could manage until I got released in June.

Release from Federal Prison

The job was easy. I hardly had to do anything. Occasionally, I would meet a customer by the loading dock, tie a mattress to a car, or exchange damaged goods. Most of the time, I sat in a small office I made for myself and made calls to let people know I was home. Most of them were girls, of course. Once I figured out the pass system, I was able to manipulate my coming and going. I found out that they couldn't refuse doctor or lawyer passes, so I became a hypochondriac with all sorts of "aches and pains."

I also found a nice little restaurant in the hospital where I spent my second day home, so I would go "to the hospital" so I could meet people and eat. I did the same thing with my lawyer. I'd have regular "legal or doctor consults" and go to a hotel not far away for a two to three-hour stay, then go back to the lawyer or doctor's office, and call the halfway house to say I was coming back. All the secretaries knew that if the halfway house staff called to check on me, (which they did once in a while), they were to say "he's in with the doctor, (or lawyer)," and that they'd have me call right back. Then they would call me on a cellphone I had and I'd go back to the office and call in. It worked well.

Since I didn't want to pay them the 25%, I never put in for furloughs. Eventually after about a month, I went to work back in New York. The first job I was on, was in the Bronx, at the new Yankee Stadium. My dad was the saw man for the job, so he got me in. I'd take the bus from Newark at 5 a.m. The bus stop was notorious for armed robberies and hookers. I never got robbed, that's all I'm saying.

I'd get into the city and take the subway to 166th Street station, walk down to street level, meet my dad for coffee, go to work, and at the days end, my dad would drive me home to his house. I'd eat, and then he would drive me to Newark to the halfway house. I had to be back by 7 p.m. every night, unless I had a "doctor" or "lawyer" appointment.

While I worked at the furniture warehouse, my cousin introduced me to a girl named Danielle. We hit it off from the start and became acquainted very soon after our first meeting. We'd frequently meet at my cousin's apartment and spend several hours together. She quickly became my driver, my lover, and my friend. We spent a lot of time together.

The Yankee Stadium job came to a close when the general foreman and his crew, my dad included, were all scheduled to work on the new World Trade Center building. I couldn't go due to strict rules against newly released felons. You had to be seven years clean, and I didn't meet that criteria. But as luck would have it, my childhood best friend was running a job over on 61st and 1st in Manhattan, so he put me on that job. It was still in the basement level of production, so I knew I'd be there for at least six to seven months.

I even got him to tell the halfway house people that I worked on Saturday, so I could get out on Saturdays, and just chill out. I'd still leave the halfway house like I was going to work. I even dressed for work but carried my backpack with clean clothes I had brought while at the furniture warehouse. I'd take the bus into the city, get off at Port Authority, and change in the bathroom. I had to go to the city so that when I called in to check in with the staff, the caller ID would show a 212 number, indicating by the area code that I was in New York City.

It was so early in the morning, and I really had nothing to do. I'd walk over to 44th Street to a little bar that had an early morning breakfast. I'd go in and eat like a king. I'd read the paper and watch all the tourists and early morning drunks come in.

This is the place I had my first drink after nine and a half years of prison. I had a Guinness and a rocks glass of Crown Royal. I remember the sound of the two glasses as they touched down on the coasters. I sat there and stared at them considering whether or not I really wanted them. I sat so long just looking at them, that finally the bar manager came over and asked me in his Irish brogue, if everything was okay.

I absent mindedly said, "I haven't had a drink in ten years."

"Off the wagon, are we?" He sounded like a mischievous leprechaun.

"No, I've been in prison for the past ten years." He didn't even look surprised.

Besides my Saturday morning excursions, I also found out that passes to church couldn't be refused either. So, I found a church on Central Avenue in downtown Newark and took the bus there every Sunday. My true intention had nothing to do with the house of God though, and much more to do with the house of pancakes that was a block away. I'd go and have breakfast there every Sunday morning.

On occasion, I'd also have breakfast dates. Then before returning to the halfway house, I'd go to the church and grab a mass sheet to prove I had gone. I spent my four months in the halfway house in this fashion. The four months went quick.

FAMILY LIFE – TRYING TO DO GOOD

I got released from the halfway house on June 8, 2007 and Danielle picked me up. By this time, we had become an item of sorts. She even introduced me to her twin daughters, Shauna and Brandy.

I went to my dad's, dropped off my belongings, and went out to celebrate my release. About a week later, my dad threw a big welcome home party for me. There was lots of home cooked food, friends from the past, and a girl who had a secret crush on me. We partied into the wee hours of the night, ate, and laughed.

I started spending weekends over at Dani's house, hanging out with her, and the kids, but I also played the field with a few other young women, including the girl with the secret crush.

I'm not sure how it happened, but eventually I started spending more and more time with Dani and the girls, until finally due to economic and comfort reasons, we moved into a beautiful old historic farmhouse in Clifton, New Jersey. It was huge, with two fireplaces, a two-car garage, two bathrooms, two bedrooms and a master bedroom along with an office. It was a really nice place.

But after several months there and finding out it had to be kept original, I backed out of buying it, and we found an apartment over on First Street in Clifton. We stayed there several months until the landlord decided they wanted to move back in, because their plans to move to Miami fell through. We had to leave on short notice. We ended up finding a really nice apartment on Union Avenue in Clifton, and we moved in, and got on with family life.

From the beginning, Dani's daughters, Brandy and Shauna, became very close to me. I helped them pick up their grades, went to school functions, plays and teacher meetings. I tried my very best to be a dad to them. We played all kinds of games, outside it was kick ball, or me plotting them against each other for some competition I'd invent inside. We'd play fight or play WII, tabletop games, or watch movies together; school and education stuff always came first though.

As the first year passed, all our lives came together in a way that ran smoothly without too many bumps or hiccups. The second year ran even smoother, as we really came together as a family unit. I worked in the city as a carpenter building high-rise units. Dani worked part time at a pharmaceutical company that she used to work for when she was younger. The girls went to school and all was well. Everybody was happy.

2007 and 2008 went on like this. Then '09 rolled in. Just like the rest, it started out uneventful. As it is with human nature, we started to live beyond our means and my old lifestyle started to seep back in. I started to sell some weed here and there. It quickly turned into a business of its own real fast. Then came the coke. And when I was prescribed pills for pain for a fall I had taken while on vacation, instead of using the medicine, (for fear of catching a habit like so many people I was hearing about), I started to sell them also, instead. I had also got involved in lending money to a guy along with a partner of mine, so between the drug money and the VIG (interest on loan), I was keeping my new family's head above water while I indulged my own seedy activities on the side, including go-go bars, etc. The extra cash was very welcome, to say the least.

After the fall I took while on vacation in the summer of '08, I worked until May 2009 when I couldn't do my job any longer, because of the pain. I collected unemployment. Dani and the girls weren't used to me being home all the time, so I think I was getting in the way a lot.

The guy my friend and I lent the money to, wasn't making good on his loan, and we came up with a few other ideas to collect the money. One of those included taking over a small catering hall and restaurant that he owned. We figured since the guy was into us for 70 grand, we would take over his business on Friday, Saturday, and Sunday nights, but not to serve food. Our ambitions were bigger than that. We wanted our own private nightclub, and we got it by taking over the catering house.

His restaurant could hold about 500 people, so we brought in popular DJs who had big followings and partied like rock stars. Dani wasn't happy that I was spending my weekends at a club drinking and hanging out with a bunch of younger girls, but it was for the money. I would tell her, we'd fight about it, but in the end, I'd always do what I wanted anyway. I could be selfish that way. I felt as long as I was paying the bills and taking care of her, and the girls, then I could just do whatever I wanted.

When I was home, our family life seemed pretty good. I loved doing things with the girls and Dani and I were home every night for dinner. I did homework with Shauna and Brandy. We played games and practical jokes on each other. It was a far cry from the cell I spent the last nine-and-a-half-years in.

While I was living this family life, I was also trying to mend the relationships with my daughter, Jackie, who I had become estranged from, while doing my prison sentence. I tried to rekindle our daddy-daughter relationship, but now at fifteen years old, she wasn't the same little girl I left behind back in '98 when I got busted as a mob enforcer. She had grown physically as well as mentally and she wasn't really interested in me, or my wanting to rekindle our family from days gone by. What she was interested in, was my money. Which at first, due to love, guilt and wanting to see her, I gave freely. This continued until she pushed too far by taking, and never spending any time with me. I had to tell her "No time, no dime." She never called me again.

So, while I couldn't mend my relationship with Jackie, I had to build ones with Shauna and Brandy. I felt like God had given me double of what I lost, (like Job in the Bible). The only problem was that I was fighting with God, and hadn't really talked to Him in many, many years.

It was from March 2007 when I met Dani, that I made a family with her, Shauna, and Brandy. We had ups, we had downs, but we enjoyed our little family, including our crazy dog Simba, whom I adored. But our family life would eventually come to an end on December 4th, 2009. In between those two times, I got pulled back into a lifestyle that undoubtedly, would catch up with me once more.

KITCHEN EQUIPMENT

I stopped at the Home Depot and picked six of the youngest, strongest looking Mexican men out from the crowd. I pulled the door to the minivan open. "Get in," I said. Several others tried to jump in with them, and I yelled "Get the hell out now, or you can all get out!" The ones I had picked obviously understood some English, because they pushed the three who had jumped in, out roughly, and yelled some things at them that I assume weren't pleasantries. I slammed the door shut and drove to a restaurant up on a hill off of Route 3 in Clifton, New Jersey.

The road to the restaurant was guarded at the entrance by a ten-foot-tall statue of Jesus looking up to the heavens with his arms stretched skyward. I pulled onto the narrow roadway that wound up at the top of a hill. I noticed the Mexicans crossing themselves at the sight of the stone Jesus. They touched their thumb to their foreheads, down on their chest, then left shoulder and finished on their right. It was all backwards in the mirror.

At the top of the hill, stood a small monastery with a large track of land. I knew it well cause Dani's daughters, Brandy and Shauna went to the affiliated school, Saint Benedict's in Clifton, and this is where they held their summer picnics and flea markets. I even ran the beer tent one year. I had to smile to myself at the memory. I had gotten a little tipsy and was flirting with some of the moms whose kids went to the school. I even winked at a nun who blushed and smiled.

We turned left, away from the monastery, and into a big parking lot where I made sure nobody was around. I parked the van by the back door that led to the catering hall kitchens. "Wait here, I'll go open the door." I got out, walked around to the front, and opened the door with the key I had. I walked through the empty front foyer, through the dining area, through a doorway, and into the dark kitchen. I went to the back door, opened it, and yelled over at the van, "Come on, let's go. Bring the tools and the generator." They jumped out like a well-trained team of DEA agents carrying tools, sawzalls, flood lights, hammers, crowbars and extension cords. "Set up the generator out here, run the cords inside, and let's get to work." I had already instructed them to cut every piece of equipment out of the three kitchens in the catering hall.

This was one of Alfonso's restaurants that him and his friend were getting started on the waterfront in Jersey City. Me and my partner went there with a letter I had him type up that stated that he, Alfonso, gave us permission to take and sell all the kitchen equipment for him.

Something told me a year ago that lending money to this guy Alfonso was a bad idea, mostly because he was so desperate. I knew the game well. He asked for a large sum, thinking he would be able to pay the VIG (interest), and then later argue that he didn't know it was interest. He would belly ache and complain, come up short, and try not to pay anymore. When you came up against clients like this, you had to rule with an iron fist, or they would just stiff you if you let them. So, the night before, I decided to make myself clear and paid him a visit at work.

Kitchen Equipment

My partner and I had driven to the huge restaurant by the pier, which also served as a nightclub, and we ate dinner, and had a few drinks. I found out that Alfonso was indeed in the kitchen cooking, so before we left, I made my way through the crowd, to the kitchen. I pushed open the door and walked into the brightly lit kitchen. It was a beehive of activity; waiters were loading trays with plates; prep cooks were preparing bowls of salad; chefs were at grill and sauté stations; people were deep frying items I couldn't make out.

I stopped about four feet into the huge kitchen and scanned the room. I saw Alfonso before he saw me. He was busy chopping something up. I walked over. He saw me as I made my way towards him. Neither of us was smiling, he out of fear and me out of anger.

"I'm really busy right now. Can we meet up tomorrow?" he said, as I walked up to him.

"No. Tomorrow ain't good enough. I need to talk to you now, let's go outside."

"This isn't a good time."

"I don't give a **** about the time. Get outside now." I walked toward him and he moved toward a door at the back of the kitchen. We went out into the night air. It smelled like steak, onions, fries, and seaweed. A few yachts were moored by the dock. I noticed them slightly bobbing up and down. The muffled sounds from inside, filtered outdoors. I pulled the paper out of my pocket. "Here, sign this," I said.

"What is it?" he said, looking worried.

"It's permission to take all the equipment from the place in Clifton," I said. His face turned white.

"I- I -I – I can't sign this. I'll be responsible for that stuff to the bank," he stammered.

"Listen, you're signing it either with ink or blood, your choice," I growled. Then pulled out a pen and pushed it through the air toward him. He looked at that pen as if it were a cobra in my hand. I looked at him with a glare that would have scared the devil himself. He took the pen and signed. I folded the paper, took my pen and walked back inside through the kitchen and back into the chatter, music, and banter of the restaurant atmosphere.

My partner was standing by the hostess's podium flirting with a cute blond, who I assumed was the hostess. "You ready?" I said as I walked past him and pushed my way through the front doors and out into the yellow lights that glowed down onto the front of the building.

"How'd it go?" he asked, as he caught up to me and we made our way to his Navigator.

"How do you think it went?" I said sarcastically. We walked quietly to the truck, got in, and left. "I'll go tomorrow with a bunch of Mexicans and cut everything out." Removing the kitchen equipment was one way of retrieving some of the money we had loaned him.

Outside the restaurant the next morning, the generator kicked on. I saw light engulf darkness inside, as the flood lights came to life. A few Spanish words were yelled out, and I heard the clatter of the sawzalls start up. I could hear the teeth of the blades biting into metal in the kitchen. I stood there for a second calculating my next move. *First, empty the main kitchen, then the upstairs one, and finally, the one in the basement.* I would then bring a U-Haul truck in and take it all to my buyer.

I went to the van, made a call on my cellphone, and smoked a joint. "I'm here and I'm all set up. Yeah, they're cutting stuff out as we speak. I'll call you later." I hung up with my friend and smoked as I texted a few messages. When I was done, I walked into the kitchen. The lights were bright and the halogen bulbs were actually radiating heat. The smell of old grease, rotten food, and burning metal all mixed together in an angry assault. I looked around at the filth that was underneath the stoves, the refrigerators and prep tables. It was disgusting. I couldn't believe I had eaten here, I wanted to puke. I wondered why the Health Department had never flagged it. I gave instructions to get everything outside in the driveway. They all just shook their heads and kept working.

I walked over to the granite topped bar with hopes of finding a fully stocked bar. As I looked around, my hopes of an early morning drink went south, along with my wishing to stock my own bar at home. I walked behind the bar to see if any bottles of whiskey or vodka had been left behind. Surprisingly, I found two half gallons of gin, and two bottles of some mixer liquor. I put them on the top of the bar, so I'd remember to put them in the van before I left.

I walked back around to the front of the bar thinking that I'd have the Mexicans cut out all the ice boxes, sinks, and bottle holders. I turned to the double wide staircase that led to the second floor and the ballroom/dining room for parties. I climbed the carpeted stairs to the top. As I made it to the top level, I could see through the spindles that tables and chairs were left behind. In my mind I calculated what that meant, extra cash.

I took in all the stainless-steel equipment and categorized it with what I saw in the main kitchen. I went through two French doors onto a medium sized roof top patio. I walked out and looked over the parapet wall down to the parking lot. Then I stared out over the August lawn from up on this roof. I could see all the way to New York City.

As I descended the stairs, the sounds of the sawzalls grew louder and so did the sound of the guys talking. I walked into the main kitchen and to my delight it was almost empty, only two pieces of large kitchen equipment were still by the door and several stainless-steel shelves were being cut off the wall. Once that kitchen was emptied, I took them upstairs, showed them the prep kitchen and an office. I instructed them to cut it all out and bring the office safe down along with the desk filing cabinet, a fax copy machine, the TV, and a few cases of wine glasses I had found.

Down in the basement, it was sectioned off with makeshift walls and piles of old chairs, tables and miscellaneous junk. It reminded me of an old cowboy movie where the towns people would block the entrance of the town with wagons, barrow wells and whatever else they could throw onto the pile. I flashed my light across the entire area of the first section. I walked carefully deeper and deeper into the back of the basement. I felt like a tomb raider exploring a tomb of an Egyptian junkman, thinking to myself the whole time, *one man's trash is another man's treasure.*

I came to a wall with a freezer. It was center smack dab in the middle of the basement. The floor all around the freezer was covered with about an inch of water. I stepped gingerly up to the freezer door and reluctantly pulled on the cold steel handle. It was slightly heavy but swung open easy enough. The smell wasn't as bad as the bathrooms upstairs, but it was definitely a close second.

My light fell onto something so rotten that it no longer was recognizable as its former self, just a black and gray blob sat there on the shelf. The smell was that stale freon-type smell mixed with rotted food. The musty tang in the air was of a quality that made me back out, but not before I caught something moving on the floor. I saw it in my peripheral vision in the dimness of my light's beam. I swung the light onto the movement and to my disgust, I was staring at hundreds of maggots crawling, slithering and wigging their fat white bodies over some old portion of meat. I looked for any sign that this bounty for the maggots' feast was a person but found none. I stepped out and shut the freezer door.

I made my way back upstairs disappointed at finding nothing of any real value. I spent the rest of the day overseeing the extraction of all the equipment that could be cut out, and then carried out.

I called my partner, who was a straight guy, but wanted to be a gangster as long as it didn't get him in trouble. "Listen, everything is out and sitting in the driveway. I need your credit card to rent a truck so I can grab the stuff. Meet me at the gas station on the 46 in Lodi. I already reserved one, okay?" I said all this as he listened.

"Okay, I'll be there in an hour," he said, and we hung up.

By day's end I had all of the stuff from the three kitchens emptied out and stacked in the side driveway next to the building. I had the Mexicans cover it all with tarps, load all the tools up and drove them back to the Home Depot where I got them from. I finished my day with a drink and some satisfaction knowing that no one was gonna "get over on me" and that I would recoup some of my money.

I PULLED ME BACK IN

If a dog just barks, and never bites, it isn't feared. Sometimes, in life, words only get you so far, at least when you're trying to collect money. This whole restaurant debacle had started because I had dipped my toe into the pool of the criminal world once again after trying to convince myself that I was out. I pulled me back in!

When the inevitable started to happen, and Alfonso started coming up short almost every week, my admonitions fell on deaf ears, so I had to implore a forceful tactic before I resorted to violence, because if history was any indicator of trying to collect money from a guy in the hospital, I knew it just didn't happen. After the equipment illustration, which was that lesson to show him who was calling the shots, he fell back in line for a while, but it didn't last long, and once again I found myself torn between being creative or sending him to the hospital.

I thought of my last ten-year sentence I had just come home from, (and which was extended because of the use of violence), and I went to my cerebral rolodex and flicked through my known criminal counterparts. I was considering which of them had hands in schemes that could possibly benefit me and help with this situation.

I quickly came upon my ex-Uncle Raymond who always had some sort of shadiness going on. We met at a pool hall and exchanged pleasantries, then got right to the crux of my dilemma. He explained that he did indeed have an opportunity for us both to make a score (money). It had to do with credit cards and running up large bills under 10,000 and collecting the monies from the owners of whatever businesses were willing to work with us. He explained it in detail, and we agreed to work together.

The scheme worked like this. My uncle would come into the business for four days straight, three times a day and bang out (swipe) cards for amounts under $10,000. Anything over alerted the IRS or government somehow. The owner had to be in on it, because he had to retrieve the money once the credit card companies paid into the business account. A few days later, for his part, the owner would garnish 40%, my uncle for his part would also make 40%, and as a finder's fee, I'd receive 20%.

Three swipes a day, for four days, each just under $10,000, and we could be in upwards of a $100,000. I would pick up 20 Gs for an intro, plus I would take half of Alfonso's 40% to pay myself back for what he owed. Win, win in my book. I made the intro. They made business, and I collected the money. Everybody was happy.

I lowered Alfonso's VIG (interest), and was making a few other moves, setting up crimes for my uncle. I was selling my drugs, collecting unemployment, which paid my child support, and living life. All was good, or at least I thought it was good, that is, until I got a call one day from Alfonso. A few months had gone by and he wanted to talk to see if we could do the credit card thing again right away.

My Spidey-senses went up and on high alert. I smelled a rat. I called my uncle after repeated calls from Alfonso. We met, and I told him how Alfonso wanted to do it again. We agreed on a date.

A few days later, I was home having lunch and the doorbell rang and my dog started barking. I got up from the kitchen table, went to the living room, and I peeked out the front window. It was my uncle standing on the top step to the front door.

He looked fidgety, stressed, and anxiety ridden. Something else was weird about him, he had shaved his head and face, and I didn't see his car anywhere. Something was up. I opened the front door and greeted him, "Hey Bubba, come in."

He stepped into the living room and blurted out, "I think I'm being followed."

"What," I said, curiously.

"I don't know if it's something we did or if it's something I did elsewhere, but I know I'm being followed." He looked shaken as he said it.

I replied, "Okay, well cancel any and everything, don't do nothing. Can you leave town for a few days?"

"Yes, that's exactly what I'm going to do. Me and my girlfriend are going to go to AC for the rest of the week, I'll be back Monday." He left and I went into my bedroom to clear out any and all illegal substances. I hid everything just in case I got picked up. Alfonso called me again to see if it was a go. I told him no, and that I'd get back in touch with him when I was ready.

The days went by, and I was running around doing my own thing. My uncle came back to town and asked to meet. We met at the pool hall. I pulled into the parking lot and saw my uncle's Caddie parked by the front door. I shut the car off, threw the keys on the floor under the front driver's seat, (as was my habit over the years), and repeated the mantra that went with the habitual movement, *the keys go with the car.* I stepped out into the brisk November air, took a deep breath and pushed the car door shut.

I pulled the tint covered glass door open. Right away, I heard the collision of balls from around the room. It was an unmistakable sound to anyone who has ever been to a pool hall. Music filled the large room. The lights were dim except for the ones that hung directly over the pool tables illuminating the green felt and reflecting a shine off the polished balls. A few guys sitting up above the floor at some tables overlooking the hall looked my way. The dim light and smoke-filled atmosphere hid their faces.

I stopped a few feet into the hall and scanned the room for my uncle. I saw him a few tables back to the right at an eight-foot table shooting by himself. I made my way over to him. We exchanged hellos while he shot a few more balls. I sat down on a couch that lined the wall behind him. "You want a drink?" he asked.

"No, I'm good. What's up," I replied.

"Okay listen, I can't figure out why I was being followed, or if I'm still being tailed, so if you want, you can go to Alfonso's by yourself."

I didn't even hesitate. "Okay, I'll set it up for this coming weekend. Just give me the cards."

"All right, you in a hurry?"

"No."

"Wait here."

He walked away from the table he was shooting at and went to the back of the hall where it was darker. The overhead lights hadn't been clicked on yet there. I watched him over in the darkness like a shadow. He sat on a couch in the back, leaned over, got up and came back. He sat next to me on the couch and handed me a stack of credit cards. It was about as thick as a deck of playing cards wrapped in a rubber band. I took it and put it in my pocket.

We spoke about a few details, and I left, got back in my car, and drove home. I hid the cards in my dresser, then texted Alfonso and told him to meet me the next day. We met and made plans to meet at his restaurant on Thursday, Friday, Saturday, Sunday to bang out a bunch of cards. It was Tuesday and I had two days to kill before I met him, so I ran around and sold my drugs, drank, and chilled. Christmas was right around the corner, so I was excited to make a score.

SECOND SWIPE

Thursday came and I met Alfonso at the restaurant early, around 9 a.m. I parked in the front. It was early, so there were no other cars parked on the street. I got out, walked around the car, and took a deep breath of the brisk morning air. The sky was clear, and the air was fresh and clean. I filled my lungs to capacity and let out a long sigh-filled breath.

I stepped up on to the curb, took two steps across the sidewalk and looked into the dining area of the place through the French door's square windows. The joint was empty, dark and quiet. Even from where I stood outside, I could tell that the silence inside was deafening. I tried the door handle, it was locked. I tapped on the glass. My knuckles hit the cold clear pane three times and the sound broke into the room like an assault on the stillness.

I saw movement out of the corner of my eye, it was Alfonso. He came through an archway that led from the dining room to the front entrance where the register was, and a section to wait for a table and to hang coats. He walked toward the door and opened it from the inside. He pushed it open, and I walked in.

Immediately, I noticed the smell of smoke mixed with food cooked yesterday. The aromas lingered in the air, the carpets, and the drapery. The smoke smell came from a brick oven in the back that he used to make thin crust pizza. Alfonso shut and locked the door behind us.

We exchange hellos, but what struck me as eerie were his next words. As we walked through the archway, he asked me, "Where's Bubba, why didn't he come?" I knew right then and there that he was setting me up.

There's no doubt now in my mind that I should have walked out, but greed being what it is, I stayed and countered his question with my own and then some. "Why you asking about Bubba? Just be lucky I'm here to do this for you. Be lucky I came to bail you out, how about that!" He looked nervous as he walked through the entrance to the other side of the counter where the register sat.

I didn't waste time with idle chitchat. I pulled out an Altoids breath mints tin filled with plastic cards. The cache of cash was only a swipe away. I opened the tin, and with the aptitude of a well-practiced magician, I used my thumb to push a card forward, as if I were ready to perform a trick. I pushed the card toward Alfonso and said, "Here." Alfonso looked at me like I was offering him a poison apple, or a cyanide pill. "Come on, let's go! I don't know how to use that," I said, referring to the register.

"How much should I put for the charge?" he asked as he grabbed the card.

I said a number, "$4,758." He stepped up to the machine, punched in the numbers on the touch screen, swiped the card, and stood there. Two seconds later, the machine came to life and a white and yellow piece of paper stacked one on top of the other came out like a tongue, and then curled up like a party blow horn. The machine fell silent.

Alfonso grabbed the paper and tore it off on the metal serrated teeth at the face of the opening. He handed me the card and receipt. Give me a pen, I said. He handed me a thin, white, Bank of America pen. I took it and wrote on a small scrap of paper $4,758. "Good, okay. I'll see you later, we still have swipes to make."

I turned and walked back through the archway, to the dining room, over to the French doors I came in through, and out to my car. I got in and drove away thinking to myself, *where are the cops, are they parked doing their surveillance, or where was Alfonso hiding the wire? He was so obvious about recording me.* Not only was I thinking this, but I could feel it too. I could feel something very wrong with this.

I still went back the next day. As planned, all weekend, we racked up close to $50,000 worth of swipes on this round. The money should have been filtering into his bank account from the various banks by Monday or Tuesday. I waited patiently all-day Monday, and late into Tuesday afternoon, before I texted Alfonso. My text read, "what time are you meeting me?" His reply was "nothing yet."

Wednesday came. I waited impatiently until 12 noon and texted him again, "what's up." His text reply was a repeat, "nothing yet." I waited until about 4 p.m. and hit him with another text, "anything happening?" "Nothing," was the one word reply I received.

I called my uncle and met him at the pool hall. He explained to me that sometimes the credit card company catches the false cards and stops payment, so it could be a bust. He also told me to make Alfonso give me his bank statements for transactions over the last three days. Thursday morning at 8:30 a.m., I texted Alfonso, "go to the bank and get a statement for last two days and meet me at the softball field at 9:30 a.m." His reply, "okay, but 10 a.m." I replied, "fine."

I was sitting in my car waiting by 9:45. I wanted to cruise the street that circled the park to see if any cops were staking it. I saw an old couple walking the track that circled the park, they looked too old to be cops. Then I spotted a young guy walking a dog. The dog looked more like a cop than the guy did. The dog even looked at me dubiously with suspicion in his big brown eyes as I drove slowly past them. When I was satisfied that I didn't care any longer, I parked by the softball field and got out of my car.

I crossed the street to the park and watched a car come up the street. It was chilly out and the light breeze was brisk, but I could still feel the heat from the sun's rays hitting my face. I looked up at the sun and squinted at its brilliance. I closed my eyes and just stood still for a moment as the sun heated up my skin. It felt so good. And for a second, it took me to a far-off place where all was right, all was good. The horn beeping jolted me back to reality.

I looked back toward the street and saw Alfonso's Mercedes wagon parked at the curb. He looked at me from behind the driver's wheel and held up a finger to indicate one minute. I noticed the phone to his ear held with his other hand. I didn't gesture back, I just stared at him hoping he could read my thoughts. Obviously, he couldn't, cause if he could, he would have put the car in drive and sped away and never looked back. My thoughts were filled with violent scenes of me beating him to a bloody pulp, stomping, kicking, and punching him … all culminating with a bullet to the head.

He got out, walked over, "Traffic is so bad over on Clifton Avenue, I thought …" I cut him off.

"Did you bring the statement," I said dryly.

"Yes," he said, as he reached into his pocket and pulled it out holding it out towards me. I took it and unfolded it. "See, I told you nothing came in. I wouldn't cheat you," he whined.

"I doubt you would, but money makes people do stupid **** all the time. Sometimes it don't hit, the credit card company must have put a stop to your payments. Call them and find out what's up," I said.

"Call them, why would I call them?" he asked with a wince.

"Cause if you don't it will look suspicious, that's why."

"Okay, I'll do it when I get to the restaurant," he said.

"On another note, you got my money?"

"Yes, I got most of it," he said.

"Listen, I'm going to lower it starting next week and it will come off the principle, and in 24 months you'll be off the hook," I said matter of factually. He looked shocked.

"What about all the monies I've paid so far?"

"Listen, you know when you took the money that you were paying a VIG weekly. Don't try to get slick with me and say you didn't know. You knew exactly what the deal was, so stop trying to get over and stop testing me or you're going to be sorry." He stammered on for a minute until I concluded our meeting by taking the G note ($1,000) he had, and left with a, "see you next week, unless that money comes in!"

I walked away. He followed at a distance. I crossed the street and got in my car just as he got into his. I passed him on the opposite side of the street. He looked up at me, and I nodded at him, and pulled away.

I called my uncle and told him about the bank statement. He said he thought it was a wash, so I moved on. I had a ton of other stuff going on, so I concentrated on my stuff all week. Between Dani, and the girls, and my illegal ventures, I was keeping busy for sure.

GET DOWN! GET DOWN!

It was December 4, 2009. At 6:17 a.m., a smashing sound woke me and my dog started barking. I rolled off of my six-inch pillow top memory foam mattress, and my feet made contact with the floor as my hand reached toward the dark corner by my bed. Even in the dark, my hand hit its mark as if the lights were on. I felt the wood handle of the bat touch my skin. My hand wrapped around it, and I felt the 32-ounce Louisville Slugger's weight lift off of the floor. I let it hang at my side as I walked around the bed. "What was that," Dani asked, as she sat up in bed.

"I don't know, go find out," I said jokingly. I could see her expression in the dim light from the window. She looked scared, but more so concerned. Her motherly instinct was on high alert. She wanted to get to the girls in the next room above all else. I pulled the bedroom door open and walked out toward the noise.

Outside my bedroom door was a makeshift office and homework niche for the girls with two desks, two computers, two of everything. The hardwood floor was cold. After four steps, I was on carpet. The noise of cracking wood filled the air along with the dog barking at the door. I raised the bat up and thought to myself, *somebody was really stupid trying to break into my house.*

The door blew open, the dog jumped back and I stepped forward. "Get down, get down, get down!" It didn't register. At first, I saw three to four people standing in the doorway, half in the foyer, half in the living room. They were pointing something at me. I looked down onto my bare chest and stomach and saw a bunch of little red dots. I let the bat drop to the floor knowing that me, the bat, and the dog put together, were no match for those little red laser guided dots that were emanating from the guns pointed at me. "Get down, get down now!" I got down onto the carpet. They burst through the door. One of them cuffed me, as another one stood there cursing, "Don't you move or I'll ******* shoot you. Don't you ******* move or I'll shoot you."

I noticed two things in those moments on the floor. One, was the carpet fresh stuff Dani used to vacuum with, smelled really great, and the other was that these guys boots were polished to such a shine that I could actually see myself in the tip of the cop's boots. The reflection sort of looked like a fun house mirror, or one of those small mirrors that are on the bigger rear-view mirrors on the side of a car.

I heard a cop to the side of me shout, "Get down, get down!" I turned my head to see Dani with a shocked look on her face, lying down on the floor next to me. I noticed the tears welling up in her big beautiful eyes. She was shocked, to say the least. The cops stood us up and sat us down on the new couch I had just bought just two weeks ago.

"My kids, where are my girls?" Dani demanded.

A detective asked, "Can you call somebody to come pick the girls up?"

I replied "Yes, call my father." And I proceeded with the number.

Another cop made the call as the detective told Dani that a female officer was with them in the bedroom. A moment later, he reported, "It's going to be okay; John's father will take them and you'll see them later. Just stay calm for them, okay?" Dani just shook her head and looked at me for answers.

I just said, "It's going to be okay, Dan, don't worry. It's going to be okay." I knew better than to talk in front of the cops.

My dad was there in ten minutes, he only lived around the corner. He came in, looked at me, "You all right?"

"Yeah, I'm fine, just take the girls and the dog, okay?"

He said "Yeah, I'll call Marty when I get home. He walked to the girls' bedroom, told them to come with him, and walked back past us."

Dani said to the girls, "It's okay, girls, Mommy will see you later. Go with John and I'll see you later." Her face was red and flustered as the tears cascaded down her cheeks.

"It's going to be okay, Dan. Don't worry, we'll be fine," I said, knowing that statement was only half true. She would be fine. I was screwed for sure. All I could think was *Alfonso!*

The detective who spoke to Dani and I started speaking again to me in particular. "John, do you have any drugs or weapons in the house?"

"No," I said, trying to sound assured.

"John, listen, I'm trying to save you the mess of us ripping everything up. Do you have any drugs or weapons in the house?"

"No," was my response again.

"Okay guys, rip it up."

I watched as two burly cops walked toward the other side of the living room toward the bedrooms and kitchen. My mind was racing a thousand miles a minute. The detective was still standing right next to me looking at me with an expression that said *don't be stupid, if it's here, we'll find it and really mess your stuff up for putting us through the aggravation.*

I spoke softly and to him directly, "Hold on, I'll tell you where it's at, just don't tear up the house, okay?"

"Okay John, just tell me what and where and I'll give my word, I won't tear it up."

I started to tell him, "It's in my safe in the bedroom."

With that, he took hold of my elbow and said "Come on, show me where."

He walked me to the bedroom, we went in and I said, "It's in the closet in my safe."

"What is the combo?" he asked.

"36-22-4," I said grumbly.

An officer who was in the room with us bent down and turned the dial on my safe. I looked at the full-length mirror on the sliding closet door. I saw myself standing there looking back at me. The me in the mirror looked disappointed with the me standing at the side of my king-sized bed. I averted my own gaze knowing that I was the culprit who had caused myself to be standing here cuffed in the first place.

"Bingo," the officer at the safe said out loud.

The detective next to me said, "Bag it and tag it." Then he looked at me and asked "Any weapons, John?"

"No," it had become a patented answer, my one-word anthem, my only retort, no.

While in the bedroom, they got me dressed. They brought me back to the living room, where Dani sat with a look of utter shock on her face, tears still rolling down her cheeks. I stood there in the middle of my living room listening to the cops, FBI and the Essex County Organized Crime Task Force guys all discussing who was going to take custody of me, and what vehicle to put me into. The sound of their voices and the chatter on their police radios filled the room. I looked at Dani wanting to somehow comfort her. All I could think to do was wink and give a halfhearted smile. She mouthed the words, *I love you* and just stared at me.

"Okay, we're ready."

"We'll take John in our vehicle and you and Judy take Danielle in your vehicle," the detective in charge said. He was the same one who had been talking to us all along. They stood us up and walked us out. It was still dark outside. Black SUVs were parked in the street with little or no regard to any parking scheme. Regular patrol cars were blocking the street on both sides of my house. Their lights were on, but not the sirens. I looked around the neighborhood to see who was watching. Most people were still in bed oblivious to what was going on. A few cars passed by, the drivers slowing down, just as they would at a five car pileup. They hardly noticed the cops walking me on the other side of the SUVs.

We stopped at the second one. The cop escorting me opened the back door and helped me get in. I climbed up on to the running board and plopped backwards onto the seat trying not to sit too heavily on my own hands and arms that were cuffed behind me. I sat there waiting to be taken back to jail.

The officer shut the door, walked around to the front passenger side door, opened it, and sat there half in the truck, half out, texting someone. I watched from my vantage point. A lady officer placed Dani in an unmarked car across the street. She couldn't see me cause the SUV was parked behind hers, and across the street, plus the windows were tinted dark black. I watched as a flatbed tow truck pulled up and took both of my vehicles away. One piggy backed on the flatbed, the other towed behind it. The tow truck's flashing yellow lights mingled with the red and blue lights from the cop cars. It was a dazzling array of lights spinning and flashing across the houses and parked cars. It reminded me of a nightclub's light show, only the music here was the music of my own grievously dour dance.

Several cops came out of my front door carrying plastic bins, others were carrying the hard drives to our computers. They looked like foreign soldiers from ancient times leaving a temple with their spoils of war. I sat and waited to see flames spring up from their torches. Another officer arrived next to the SUV, opened the driver's side door, got in and said, "We're out of here, you ready?" He was talking to his partner.

His partner said "Yeah, I'm good, let's go."

The driver started the SUV and put it in drive. He pulled away slowly. At first, I watched as two more cops came out my front door, then I sat straight and resigned myself to the facts, which were that I was arrested, in custody, headed for the police station, and helpless. The whole ride I sat silently thinking to myself, trying to hold out all hope, that this bust was only for the drugs. But deep in my gut I knew Alfonso had his hand in it, and he had ratted me out.

QUESTIONING

We got to the federal building in Newark quickly. After all, the cops didn't have to worry about getting pulled over, so they could go as fast as they wanted. They brought Dani and I in at different times, put us in separate rooms, and left us by ourselves just sitting there, cuffed and alone. They stuck their heads in every so often to see if I was still there, or whether I had vanished into thin air.

I was sitting in there with my head resting on top of my hands. Upon placing me in this room they had uncuffed me and cuffed just my one hand to the table where an eye bolt protruded from the top. After a long moment alone, except for the occasional popping in of the head to say, "You okay," the head Detective came in, sat down and pushed the door shut.

The room was maybe five by five. I sat on one side of the short three-foot table and he took his place across from me. "John, I'm Detective Dimitri. I'm here to inform you of your Miranda Rights and let you know what you're under arrest for. But before we start, do you have any questions?"

"Yes, is Dani okay?" I asked questioningly.

"Yes, she's fine. She's in the next room. Don't worry, she's being treated fine," he said reassuringly.

I replied, "Thank you."

"Okay, John, are you aware of your Miranda Rights? Let me say them anyway. You have the right to remain silent. You have the right to an attorney of your choice. If you cannot afford one, one will be appointed to you by the court of law. Anything you say here can and will be used against you in a court of law. Do you understand these rights, and would you like to say anything?"

"Yes, and yes," I replied.

"Okay, what's up," he said.

"I understand you have a job to do. I'm not trying to break balls or waste your time. I have nothing else to say, other than I'd like to make a call to my lawyer."

"Okay John, I understand." He got up and left. I sat there alone for what seemed like hours until he came back, stuck his head in, and said, "I want you to know I got you on the phone talking. He held up a small recorder, pushed play and my voice came to life with the following words: *Hey, I just saw the chef. He's supposed to meet me later with 10 Gs. I'll call you after I see him.* He clicked the recorder off, and said, "See."

My reply was, "I'd like to speak with my attorney, please." Detective Dimitri pulled the door shut and left.

He came back twice more to say different things. I just continued to ask for my lawyer. Finally, an officer came in and said "John, I'm Detective Mayer. I need to take a statement from you about the drugs." He placed a small recorder on the table, hit play, and said,

"This is Detective Mayer of the Essex County Drug Task Force. On 12-4-09 at 9:15 a.m. this statement is from, state your name, please ..." He looked at me and I just took over.

"My name is John A. Paladino. Social security number XXX-XX-XXXX. I live at ... Clifton, New Jersey. The drugs that were found in my house were mine and mine alone. Danielle Preston had no knowledge of any drugs. The drugs were mine and mine alone. Thank you, have a nice day."

He said, "Now, that's how you do it." He clicked off the recorder, got up and stepped out. I sat alone once again.

About ten or fifteen minutes went by, and Detective Mayer stuck his head in. "Hey John, I just want to tell you I seen a lot of tough guys sit in that same seat and rat somebody out or try to put the blame on their girlfriend. I respect what you did." I just nodded my head at him as he pulled the door shut. I thought to myself, *I could never be a rat ever!*

Later that day I found out that the cops, had arrested me, Dani, my uncle, my partner, my cousin, and several others that were involved at different levels of different crimes, whether it was with the drugs or the credit cards. We all got busted because of the one person who wasn't arrested, Alfonso!

COUNTY JAIL

We were all transferred over to "The Green Monster," also known as Essex County Jail, in Newark, New Jersey; one of the toughest counties on the east coast. I was brought in and processed, along with everybody else. It was Friday, December 4, 2009, and all I cared about was getting Dani out so she could be with Brandy and Shauna. I knew there were people on the streets that were rallying at that very moment, calling lawyers, calling bondsmen, finding out bails, trying to find out charges. It was always chaos for family and the friends of the arrested from the day of arrest, until the day you got bailed out or sentenced. It was constant chaos and uncertainty.

The whole area, or the whole world for that matter, learned of the arrest because it was in every newspaper, and on every news channel, and the internet. I couldn't believe I was sitting in this bull pen with three of my now known co-defendants. I knew if we didn't bail out by tonight, we were destined to sit in a quarantine cell for the next seven days, after we sat in the intake holding tanks for the rest of the weekend.

By Sunday night, Dani, my cousin, and several others were all released, which left me, my Uncle Raymond and my partner. We sat in the bullpen, or tank, as some people call it. It is a twenty by twenty holding area with one toilet in the open and concrete benches lining the walls. It is meant to hold thirty men but is packed with fifty to sixty at any given time. Guys are stretched out on the floor, on the benches, or under the benches. Wherever there was an open and free inch, there was a body.

The tank smelled of a combination of sweat, piss, feces, bologna, vomit, and industrial strength Pine Sol. Every breath in was offensive in a new and disgusting way. I tried to inhale shallowly, but it didn't help. Nobody in that bullpen had showered or brushed their teeth for days, on top of whatever condition they had come in with.

I made it from the tank to a processing area, where you get stripped down, and your clothes are placed in a plastic bag with your name on it and hung on a revolving rack, like in a dry cleaner's shop. The clothes looked like body bags hanging with a name tag on meat hooks. I thought to myself, *I might as well be dead, cause that's all this was going to be, was dead time.* I was given a bed roll, two boxers, two T-shirts, two socks, a hygiene kit, and an orange jump suit. I was allowed to keep my own shoes.

We were fingerprinted and photographed and adorned with a plastic bracelet that was clamped to our wrist with a type of rivet. This was our ID bracelet and once it was scanned, all of our info came up; name, age, date of birth, social security number, housing unit, and charge. That bracelet was a constant reminder of the fact that liberty was no longer mine. I was now a prisoner once more.

By Tuesday, I was the last man standing out of my six codefendants; everyone else had made bail. I was trying, but I had a federal detainer, so I was stuck like Chuck. I spent fifteen months in The Green Monster waiting for my day in court, which I finally got, on January 20, 2011. I was sentenced to seven years for conspiracy to collect money, usury, (which is just a fancy name for loan sharking), and attempted credit card fraud. Part of my plea deal was to get Dani cut loose as my co-defendant. I didn't want her involved for anything I did, especially because of the girls.

My fifteen months in County was uneventful, thankfully. About a month after I got sentenced to my seven flat in state, I was taken to court on February 18th to be sentenced in front of a federal magistrate for violating my federal probation. The judge was very nonchalant when he stated that I "had no redeemable qualities" and then gave me twenty-one months on top of the seven-year sentence I had received only a month earlier.

My life-long criminal pursuits had accumulated to the point where although all of my codefendants had gotten probation and large fines, I was the only one to get any prison time. After being sentenced by the Feds to the twenty-one months, I went back to the county and waited to be shipped out to prison. I didn't have to wait long. It was only a week later that I heard my cell door being buzzed and my name being called out, "Paladino pack it up, you're 'going down' this morning."

Any convict worth his weight, knows what "going down" means when that cell door cracks at 4:30 a.m. It means leaving for prison; for better living, from an incarcerated standpoint. Better food, cheaper canteen, weights, contact visits, jobs, earning a pittance. It was an improvement.

It's funny how jail is set up to take everything away from you, but how you can gather and collect so much of nothing in such a short time. Sometimes I felt like an old lady who saves and reuses plastic bags cause it's exactly what you do when you get locked up. You save things you'd throw away or take for granted on the streets. You recycle stuff, knowing that you don't have the luxury of going to the convenient store to buy what you need. I'd have a collection of extra spoons, cups, bread, jellies, books, magazines, notepads, clothes, newspapers, bowls, etc. Prison was like being on survivor island, you learned to make use of everything around you. You create uses for every single thing you lay your hands on. Your most valued tool of choice is the prison swiss army knife, a toenail clipper.

I packed up quickly. When you leave to go to prison, you can't take anything with you except personal property like letters, pictures, legal work, and personal books. Everything else you have to leave behind for guys that don't have anything like radios, food, clothes, magazines, and any other accumulated belongings you might have stacked up while doing your time there.

CRAF TO MID STATE PRISON

I left County the last week of February and was brought to CRAF (Central Reception Assignment Facility) where you are literally stripped of everything you have. Your belongings are mailed to an address of your choice along with your clothes, if you still have any from the county. Yet even if you're in an orange jump suit it's also taken and you're left standing as naked as the day your mother gave birth. The only thing missing is the smack on the ass and the doctor that exclaims it's a boy.

> "Hands up.
> Open your mouth.
> Lift them (your genitals).
> Turn around.
> Right foot up.
> Left foot up.
> Bend over, spread them (butt cheeks).
> Now cough!"

If you're shy about your body, all your inhibitions are quickly stripped away along with everything else. You're left naked to the world, but more immediately to the several officers that are standing there stripping you and checking tattoos for any gang affiliations. It took four cops to check me out from head to toe, because I am covered in tats except for my face, head, neck or hands. I left them clean just in case I need to put a suit on in any professional capacity or meet someone for the first time and make an impression. I was aware that my size alone was already taken into consideration when people judged me, I didn't need to make myself into a walking billboard.

I sat in CRAF in substandard and draconian conditions for three weeks waiting, once again, for my name to be called at 4:30a.m. It's funny how you can hate being locked up, but thankful for the upgrade from county to CRAF and then to prison, where living can be a little more comfortable. I had nothing to pack on the morning of March 15, 2011. All I owned at this point was neatly packed in a state prison laundry bag; three brown khaki pants, three brown khaki shirts, two boxers, two T-shirts, two socks, a pair of 97 cent shoes, a handbook, one piece of paper from classification stating my term, my credits, my status (which was minimum), a description of me, date of birth, and finally destination, MSCF (Mid State Correctional Facility).

I climbed onto the Bluebird (the bus), which got its name years ago. It used to be an old school bus and was painted pale blue with grates welded over the windows and metal gates welded just in front of the first seat and behind the last seat to keep us secure in the event someone tried to escape or attack a guard.

Every time I'd ever ridden on the Bluebird, my thoughts always went to a recurring scene; one in which the bus crashed, and we couldn't get out because we were locked in it like a mobile cage, handcuffed and shackled, and the guards were knocked out and the bus caught fire. Or every time we passed over a bridge, I thought of the bus careening from side to side, then crashing through the railing and free falling down into the murky depths of the water below. Thankfully, neither of these doomsday visions came to pass over the years, despite my many trips cuffed and shackled in the back of a DOC (Department of Corrections) vehicle.

CRAF to Mid State Prison

The bus had thirty-two guys on it. Fifteen were going to SWSP (South Woods State Prison), ten were going to Leesburg State Prison, and the remaining seven, myself included, were being brought to MSCF. We pulled onto the huge military base belonging to Fort Dix and drove down long roads lined on both sides by an assortment of trees. Small dirt roads broke off from the main road into the dense tree line. Some were marked with plywood signs that stated A-7, C-10, B-1. I thought they may have been fire access roads, or military training exercise roads. Either way, I didn't really care. I just wanted to get settled in, go lift, eat better, get a few contact visits, do my time, and go home to start all over once again, for the fourth, and hopefully, the last time.

The bus pulled into a small parking lot and stopped in front of a twelve-foot-high razor wire topped fence. A guard in a one-man booth stepped out, came over to the bus, and said something to the cop driving. The other cop riding shotgun took his partner's gun and clips (bullets) and stepped off the bus. A huge sign on the fence explained what he was doing. It stated NO WEAPONS BEYOND THIS POINT. He went to the booth and stepped in, was out of view for a minute or two, then stepped out without his or his partner's guns.

He climbed back on board and said something to the driver that made him laugh. We sat there waiting for something to happen five, ten, fifteen minutes, then finally we heard it before we saw it, the motor that pulled the gate open had whizzed to life squeaking and clanking. The chain rattled and bounced loosely as it pulled the heavy gate open. The gate rumbled to a clamorous stop. The bus pulled in and stopped in front of another identical fence, where the same scene was repeated as if it were déjà vu, but first the fence we just passed through closed behind us. We were trapped in between the two mouths of the prison. We were being ingested, but luckily it was a two-way street, and the light at the end of the tunnel wasn't a train.

The second gate opened, and we drove into the prison compound. I noticed the watch tower with the guard looking down onto us from his perch in his tower. The Bluebird rolled to a stop at the side of the prison in front of a steel door. There were already cops standing outside waiting like an "unwelcoming" committee. They stood in a line parallel to the outside wall of the prison. They all had on black leather gloves, some had on dark sunglasses. All of them were trying their best to look intimidating. I've seen that look before and it always made me laugh inside, because I knew the truth that they were really the ones who were scared of guys like me, the unpredictable spontaneously violent inmates who they already knew were on the bus.

At the front of the bus on the other side of the gate, one of the transportation cops bellowed out, "Listen up for your name. When I call you, step up, give me your number, and date of birth. Get off the bus and lineup on the yellow line facing the front of the bus. Don't talk. Don't look around. Just stand there and keep quiet." The officer unlocked the front gate, held up his clipboard and started to call names. Each man went up and did as he was told. When my name was called, I also followed suit, gave my number, stated my date of birth, got off the bus and lined up as I was instructed.

Once the seven of us were unloaded and accounted for, we were marched inside a receiving area, taken into a side room, uncuffed and stripped down again. We emerged from the strip room, and our bags were lined up against the far wall. A coat, a cup, a spoon and a bag of hygiene products were all packed into our bags. The trustees (the prison gophers) who had prepared the bags, stood at the other side of the room looking at us to see if they recognized any of their homeboys or repeat offenders.

An officer called out our names from behind a podium. Each man got a piece of paper with a number, a letter, and another number. Mine said 7-East-21. "Pick up your bags and follow me," the officer said. We did as we were instructed. We walked out of the receiving area into a short hallway, made a left, and followed the officer down a long, polished concourse. The floor glistened in a way that if it were blue, you would have thought you were walking on water.

As we passed door after door, inmates were coming and going out of several of them, including the social services department, the education department, the storeroom, canteen, and gym. I glimpsed a peek at the gym through the twelve-by-twelve square of glass that was at the center of the door. I couldn't see much. The glass was too dirty, stained by years of dirt, sweat, paint, and the handprints of the many who had undoubtedly peered through this same little window.

The officer directed that whoever had numbers one through four were to stand against that wall. We stood there and watched the officer and the four other guys walk through a gated opening that separated the hallway. I looked back down the hallway and didn't even notice there was another gate about a hundred feet away right past the mess hall. I didn't notice it because of my interest in the gym. This is how prison was; gates and cell doors everywhere so in case of a riot the staff could try and cut the rioters off from the other areas of the jail. However, most gates just usually stayed open anyway because of the laziness of the staff members.

The officer came back and walked us down the hall and dropped each inmate at his appointed unit. I was used to this because it was now my fourth prison sentence. He stopped at seven east, which was my new home for the next whatever amount of months. The officer left me at the desk with the housing officer, Mrs. Romano. It was time to get settled into prison once more.

SETTLED IN

Mrs. Romano introduced herself, her rules, and then said, "Let's go get you settled in." She walked down the foyer to a gate. She unclipped her set of huge keys and unlocked the gate. She walked me in and said, "Twenty-one is about halfway down." I walked onto the tier and straight to my bunk. I threw my laundry bag onto the bottom bunk and took a look around.

The first person I said hello to was a white kid who was laying across his bunk fully dressed, obviously waiting to go somewhere such as school, work, or the library, etc. We introduced ourselves. "Hey, bro, how you doing, I'm Little John."

He replied "Hey, I'm Matt."

It was the meeting that would change my life forever, and in a tremendous way.

Upon entering this prison, or any prison, for that matter, I had absolutely nothing of any real value, which in prison economy, means food, cigarettes, or stamps. But as the days went on, and Matt and I became friendlier, and he made it a point to always offer me anything he had, or to contact my family for me. And at night, when he had food, he always gave me half of it. Food wasn't the only thing he shared with me either, but first, I had to learn the lay of the land, before I could accept anything else.

The sliver of time between my arrival at Midstate and my meeting Matt was filled with thoughts of grandeur. I had a few years to do, so I would whip myself into shape mentally and physically. (The spiritual aspect was not a thought in my mind yet.)

I made my way, as always, to the gym, where I knew I would become the talk of the prison by benching a lot of weight. This gym, as with this whole prison, was running on empty. All the universal machines were broken, or the cables were snapped. The only thing left that worked, and couldn't really be broken, was the Smith machine. It consisted of a large frame which had two vertical metal poles on either side with a forty-five-pound long weight bar attached to it, which allowed it to glide up and down freely. The bar had two safety hooks attached to it, and the frame had heavy metal studs sticking out, so that you could save yourself from a failed lift without getting injured.

I found a group of guys bench pressing. I stood by and watched to see who could do what and did a quick calculation on how much weight was available. The total amount was 465 pounds. There were four 45s, four 35s and four 25s and I added the two brackets with the hooks as 10 pounds each.

I asked the group of guys if I could get in on their work out, and they said okay. I laid on the bench confidently knowing that all the push-ups, pull ups and dips I had done in the Green Monster would help now. I warmed up with 135 for thirty, then did a set of 225 for twenty. Then 275 for an easy ten. Then 325 for six. Then 365 for four. Then 415 for four and finally 465 for two good ones. I got up, thanked them for letting me in, and noticed that the whole gym had been watching the new big white guy do his thing. My first month went on this way. I'd eat, sleep, and workout.

My life had deteriorated to a point where I didn't care anymore about whether I stayed in prison, lived, or died. I was lost in many more ways that I cared to recognize. I had a one-track mind and it was to learn more hustles to bring home and implement once I was released.

I found comfort around the like-minded men. I had come to Midstate begrudgingly. I wanted to go back to Rahway (EJSP) where the atmosphere was thick with tension. It was the type of tension that kept the nonsense to a minimum. Like the equivalent of circling sharks, the guys in Rahway for the most part were "men" doing tons of time; most of which would never see freedom again. This was where I felt most comfortable. These were serious guys. It was no day-care center, nor was it for the faint of heart.

I remember an incident where a guy killed another guy right in the middle of the mess hall. I watched him drag his victim over to the 50-gallon coffee tank and opened the valve on his face—pouring steaming hot coffee all over his head basically cooking his skin and melting it down his face. This was the atmosphere that I wanted to go back to; where I felt most at home.

I once heard of a story of a lion who escaped his enclosure and ran off to the hills of North Carolina, only to come back to his old cage a month later. The lion had gained his freedom but made a choice to come back to what he had always known instead. Here I was, like that lion, locked up once again in a cage I came back to willingly. A lion who didn't known that the cage was stunting him mentally and spiritually. The comfort, in my case, of a life of crime, had rocked me to sleep and kept me far from the power that I could have actually been experiencing.

Ironically, I was still drawn into conversations with my new friend Matt frequently. Matt was different than the hardened guys I was most comfortable being around. I found out that he was a Christian, but it meant nothing to me. I wasn't looking for God, nor did I want anything to do with Him. I blamed God for my life of misery and pain. I always thought of the line from Milton's, *Paradise Lost* as my motto, "I'd rather rule in hell than serve in heaven."

All the years I'd spent in prison were with the mindset that anyone who sought God in prison was weak. I thought, *if it was so important to seek Him, why didn't they seek Him on the streets? If they did, maybe they wouldn't be here now.* I had reverence for religion, but not the people. I read voraciously about all religion and philosophy, not to learn it or believe it, but instead to debate those who toted their God's flags. I went to church not to pray or confess, but only to meet friends or drop swag or messages. I had no use whatsoever for anyone's "God." I was a persecutor of Christians, Catholics, Muslims, of all who spoke of God. Yet I called myself a "spiritualist." I didn't consider myself to be an Atheist. I knew there was something out there, but whatever it was, it had no use for me, and I had none for it.

Oddly enough, at 46 years old, when I spoke with Matt though, I found interest in what he had to say about his God. I found interest in Matt's demeanor and his peace, so when he spoke, I listened.

One day Matt said he was going to start a Bible study on the unit and asked if I would like to join him. I said yes for no other reason than to show support to this young man who had continually been kind to me. The first few days, there were only about five of us. We would sit and listen to Matt tell an anecdote about an animal, or his own life as a professional soccer player. He always made it interesting and related to Jesus. I didn't bother with church on Sunday though, or male leadership on Monday. I just ate, slept, and lifted a regimented routine that, in my eyes, kept me busy and out of trouble. But something was changing.

Seventeen months into my seven-year sentence and never having before thought of God or wanting to seek Him, He was now presenting Himself to me through this young man Matt, who I was quickly becoming attached to, as well as learning from.

I DIE!

My world as I knew it, being a tough guy, a mob enforcer, a gangster, and a hardened convict with a reputation of spontaneous violent propensity, all came crashing in on Memorial Day, 2011.

I started my day as usual. I got dressed, put on my boots, brushed my teeth, washed my face, and went about my business.

Later that afternoon, as I stood in the bathroom, I noticed someone in the mirror staring at me. I spoke into the mirror, to the person staring back at me, "What are you staring at!" It was more of a statement, than a question, so I didn't expect the answer I got back. I didn't expect any answer at all. I mean after all, *I am Little John, a 330-pound menace with a resume of leaving the bodies where they lay.*

The reply came, "At you, you wretched man!" The words hung in the air for a second, but when they finally registered, they cut deep; not for their insulting value, but more so, for the truth they wielded. Those words stung my heart like poisonous darts, because it's exactly how I felt deep inside for coming back to prison for the fourth time, like a wretch.

I spun around and came face to face with the man who stood as tall as me, had as many tats as me, was bald just like me and looked as mean as I did. For a second, I saw a familiarity in his eyes, but the recognition was interrupted by the crushing blow his fist caused as it landed on my jaw. The punch took me by surprise, but I reacted in turn with my own well-placed punch.

He threw another, as did I. We stood toe-to-toe, throwing the heaviest of punches. No words were exchanged, only an occasional grunt. We beat each other unmercifully, punch after punch landing on its target heavily. I could feel the hate in my punches as I threw them, but it seemed as though the harder I hit him, and the angrier I got, my own strength started to wane. I fought more vigorously, only to sense as though he was growing stronger. I could swear I heard him say, "If God is with me who shall stand against me!"

As much as I wanted to win this fight, I felt myself growing wearier. I threw powerful punches that he answered with his own. We fought for what felt like an hour. He grabbed me and I could feel he had real strength—a strength deeper than any physical strength. I had a strength that was reaching its limits. He was fighting like a man on a mission. He was fighting as though he were on a crusade for his God. I had no God to fight for, or one who stood with me against a foe.

I started to feel like I wasn't going to win this fight. We fell to the ground where he gained the upper hand on me. He had me in a choke hold and the more I struggled, the tighter his grasp became. That's when I heard him say, "You never listened to me over the years when I came to tell you that God loves you and wants you to do good. You never understood it was me *who is you*, saved by the grace of God that wanted to save you. Now with the blood of Christ, which cleanses, I must end your life so you can continue on as a new creation in Christ."

I Die!

I heard what he was saying as I was slowly losing consciousness. I now realized all the years I had done wrong and was approached by that mysterious man who tried to stop me at the exact moment I needed it, was me, trying to save me. I now realized that I'd have to die to myself in order for Jesus to come into my life and create the new life. I couldn't obtain salvation on my own. Jesus had to do it for me.

I passed away in the arms of a Christ-filled man who wanted nothing more than to remain filled with the Holy Spirit, and to be in relationship with God and Jesus Christ. The old Little John died on Memorial Day 2011, only to have the new Holy Spirit-filled Little John emerge from the ashes of an ashtray moved from crime to Christ, with a new conscience.

The story is the greatest of all my stories. With Matt's help, God worked on me in an undeniable way.

†

It all began the night before. Another inmate and myself were talking about God and while I admitted a need for change in my life, I was vocal to confirm my doubt that it would ever happen. My reasons were solid and lined up. First, I had worked hard to establish a reputation as a "tough guy" and was not interested in giving that up, and second, I admitted that I wasn't really convinced about God anyway. I didn't plan on being one of those "desperate" guys who found God in prison.

As Vinney and I debated back and forth, I said, "Wouldn't it be so much easier if we could just ask God to move this ashtray across the table? And then, I would definitely believe in Him." We talked through the night; the ashtray only moving when Vinney moved it himself, to put ashes in it or to extinguish his cigarette.

With heavy eyes, I went to bed thinking nothing more of my bravado suggestion to God to move my ashtray. At that moment, I didn't know or understand that He could see exactly what was going on in my heart. He knew that deep down (in a place that I didn't want to show anyone else), I really desired change, peace, and to be saved from this life I had been leading. He knew I was searching. I seriously did want God to move that ashtray.

The next day, Matt was called out to get legal mail, so he asked me if I would start the Bible study by reading the Daily Bread for the day, and I agreed. The crazy part was that on that day, the group ballooned from eight guys to twenty. It was weird actually, but I pressed on, oblivious to what God was about to do. I had been attending the Bible group not because I was a Christian, but because I wanted to support Matt in his ministry. I also wanted to be sure nobody messed with Matt, so I was there for protection, almost like a bouncer. As a result, I ended up being privy to many Bible lessons and his teaching. I had to admit I found it interesting, and at times, it stirred my heart.

I confidently picked up the Daily Bread Matt had asked me to read and began reading the passages. As I attempted to read, something suddenly and unexpectedly overwhelmed my spirit. As I read those words, I felt my heart stirring and a lump form in my throat. I could see the words, but only two or three of them came out of my mouth. It was surreal. I had no idea what was happening. I tried again desperately to read and regain my composure. The whole ordeal of showing emotional vulnerability was unfamiliar territory to me. I couldn't remember the last time I cried. And publicly? Me? Never! So, before a tear could fall and with all eyes on me, I got up looking confused and out of sorts. I excused myself momentarily and headed quickly to the bathroom. It was there that the fight commenced between my old life and my new one.

Splashing water on my face, I tried my best to wash away the feelings that were flooding out of me. I spoke to myself in the mirror, "Come on John! What are you doing? Pull yourself together, you're a tough guy, a gangster. Don't cry in front of these guys, don't let your interior be exposed, don't let your armor be dented or stripped, stand strong!" I threw a few shadow punches in the air and I gathered myself together—or so I thought—and went back to the group.

I tried to joke it off by saying it was something I ate, but as I once again picked up the booklet and tried to read the words, nothing came out of my mouth but gut-wrenching sobs. There I sat, a hardened and notorious mobster, crying openly in front of the entire tier, choking out muffled words in between sobs. What in the world was happening to me?

I could see the other inmates shocked and amazed looks, trying to figure out what was going on, mouths wide open. They were just as confused as I was, watching me struggle to maintain my composure. No one uttered a word. They couldn't fathom this 300-pound "tough guy" breaking down by simply attempting to read the Word of God.

Deep down, I knew I wanted peace in my heart like I had witnessed from Matt and another Pastor that had recently visited the prison. I explained to the group, how I went to church with Matt the night before and listened to the speaker give his testimony and knew that my heart was stirred. I could no longer deny what I had observed in these men living their lives with such confounding peace, confidence and fortitude that I had never seen. I confessed that I wanted what these men had, and I realized God was sending me a clear message at that very moment that I could have it because He was listening to my heart's yearnings all along. I declared that I wanted to ask Jesus to be my personal Savior.

I got through the fellowship group and felt cleansed and peaceful. My day went on as usual, but I felt consumed with the perplexing thoughts of trying to understand what had happened. The day's events were weighing on my mind, and yet I felt great; I felt clean, whole, and happy.

That night I went to bed and just as I was dozing off to sleep, it hit me ever so clearly. I sprung up and called to Matt, (his bunk is next to mine) and said, "Bro, that was God moving my ashtray!"

My challenge to God to move an ashtray was such a foolish and miniscule task that any magician could have accomplished it. It occurred to me that God was showing—not only to me—but to all those present that day, that He could do a much greater work than move a simple ashtray. He could move a tough guy's very hard heart.

That night I got the best sleep I've had in years.

This was the undeniable day that God moved me from crime to Christ. I once was just like Saul, a persecutor of Christians. I previously had my own beliefs, which to me, meant that everyone else was wrong. I found weakness where they found strength. I saw conformity as a deficiency, when I was an outlaw. I watched them gather in peace and harmony, while I walked alone in total chaos and destruction. While Christians sang, prayed, and praised, I thought of others' demise, and condemned as many as I could.

The Saul in me thought this was how I should act, how I should think. I found no fault in my own eyes. I believed I exemplified power, strength, and my own form of righteousness, that is, until I met Christ. I didn't meet Him on the road to Damascus, but on an empty dead-end road in prison; where I sat for years at a time without seeing a way out.

My eyes were blind until the day I met Christ. He opened them and now I see more clearly than I've ever seen before. Christ touched my heart and gave me a new purpose in my soul. I went from crime to Christ and am now a new man. I now see strength in my weakness. I now sing and praise. I now pray in peace. I now uplift and encourage. I now conform and speak softly. I now have faith in Christ with all things. I now, am on mission for Christ, not a life of crime.

After being saved, I sat in prison, a new man, in all I said, did, and felt. I had approximately thirty-six months still hanging over my head, yet for reasons that no one else could figure out, I was at total peace. I now knew who saved me, and it wasn't me, but the God, who loved me all along despite me—Jesus, my Savior.

As I finished my time in prison, I learned daily to combat the inner turmoil I felt, the battle of the flesh and spirit. I knew that my spirit was willing, but my flesh was weak. My future was only as certain as my faith, yet I did not look to the future, nor did I live in the past. I tried my best to remain grounded in my faith in the present.

>What then shall we say to these things?
>If God is for us, who can be against us?
>Romans 8:31

LIFE AFTER DEATH

If you could have had a "before" and "after" photo of me, (like you see in the workout or diet advertisements), you would have seen a man's countenance change from a rugged exterior to a softer posture.

This man was me; a criminal with a serious resume spanning over the course of more than two decades—all to be wiped clean by the utterance of a few words. As much dirt as I had done in my life, and as much damage, hurt, and destruction as I committed through many years of ill will, I felt in that moment of need and want, that the words I spoke asking Jesus to come into my life were words that changed my life forever and for the better. It sounds crazy, I know, but the day I asked the Lord Jesus to save me and be my Savior was the day my soul was cleansed.

After being saved, I felt mentally and physically great. Yet, more than that, my heart and soul felt clean as if I had been turned inside out and run through a car wash. I couldn't help but tell every and anyone who would listen, that I had been saved by God's grace.

As I pen these words, I pause and think about how easy it could be to spend life in prison, if you didn't know any better. Being impulsive and acting out is the easy part. Having self-control and restraining from impulses is difficult at times. Like many criminals, my mind had become completely conditioned into thinking criminal activity was normal. In the end, we all have to live with the consequences of our own choices, and I did that, many times over. It's not until we're met with the realization of what life could be, that we begin to struggle somewhere between clinging to the comfort and the default operation we once knew and considering living a new life. For me, what "could be" started to present itself in front of me, through my dear friend, Matt. And I couldn't look away.

I openly admit that God's grace saved a sinner, but He definitely is still working on me, as there is room yet for improvement. I still have moments of anger, impatience, stubbornness, and gangster thoughts, but the real victory I experience is that I don't have to act on any of these impulses anymore. Instead, I feel like a child who wants to make his Father proud. So now I think before I speak or act because I want to make my "Father" God pleased with me. I try my very best to live with the nine fruits of the Spirit on my mind: love, joy, peace, patience, kindness, goodness, faithfulness, gentleness, and self-control. I no longer live in the dark of what could be for me. The "unknown" was revealed to me which is the power of Christ Jesus—and my heart was filled with a newfound comfort that is now the new "norm" for me.

Life has its struggles. It can be hard and cruel. But life doesn't have to be any of these negative things when all we have to do is live with Jesus in our hearts.

Today, I am a free man once more. I don't worry about the past because I have repented and I don't stress about the future because I find no comfort in what hasn't come to pass yet. My only comfort comes in the knowledge that I am filled with the goodness of

God's Spirit. I have unwavering faith and am hopeful that God will keep me grounded in Him.

I live to glorify God through such platforms as my testimony to others, whenever I can give it, and through my writings, such as this book. Could I have saved me from me? It was never my work to do. It was the victory on the cross of Calvary that completed it, long before I would ever battle between my old and new life.

I am a changed man because of Jesus and how He makes me feel and think ... and for this, I am a grateful servant of God.

ABOUT THE AUTHOR: John Paladino

John Paladino grew up on the streets of northern New Jersey. He is one of two kids from an Italian family. He began breaking the law at age ten, which eventually led to a life of crime into young adulthood and resulted in him spending the next 20 years in and out of prison. John has been called many things in his life, from hoodlum to tough guy, and more serious monikers like gangster and murderer—all of which are buried with his past since he encountered the Lord in his last stint of prison. Presently, by God's grace alone, "Little John" is now called Christian. John is also the author of *How God Moved My Ashtray, A Devotional Experience*.

For inquiries about John, please go to www.truthovertrend.com/contact and drop us a message.

IF YOU ENJOYED THIS BOOK, WILL YOU CONSIDER SHARING THE INFLUENCE WITH OTHERS?

- Share or mention the book on your social media platforms.

- Recommend this book to those in your small group, book club, Bible study, workplace, and classes.

- Pick up a copy for someone you know who would be spiritually challenged and biblically charged by this message.

- Write a book review on amazon.com, bn.com, goodreads.com, or cbd.com

FOR MORE LITERARY INFLUENCE,
PLEASE VISIT
www.5511publishing.com

www.ingramcontent.com/pod-product-compliance
Lightning Source LLC
LaVergne TN
LVHW051359080426
835508LV00022B/2902